LOYALISTS IN THE ADIRONDACKS

THE FIGHT FOR BRITAIN IN THE REVOLUTIONARY WAR

Marie Danielle Annette Williams

Published by The History Press
Charleston, SC
www.historypress.com

Front cover, bottom: *View of the Ruins of Ticonderoga Forts on Lake Champlain. Analetic Magazine*, April 1818. Courtesy of the New York Public Library.
Back cover: *Ethan Allen's Capture of Fort Ticonderoga 1775.* John Steeple Davis. New York Public Library.

Unless otherwise indicated, all images are courtesy of M.D.A. Williams.

First published 2023

Manufactured in the United States

ISBN 9781467152068

Library of Congress Control Number: 2022951589

Notice: The information in this book is true and complete to the best of our knowledge. It is offered without guarantee on the part of the author or The History Press. The author and The History Press disclaim all liability in connection with the use of this book.

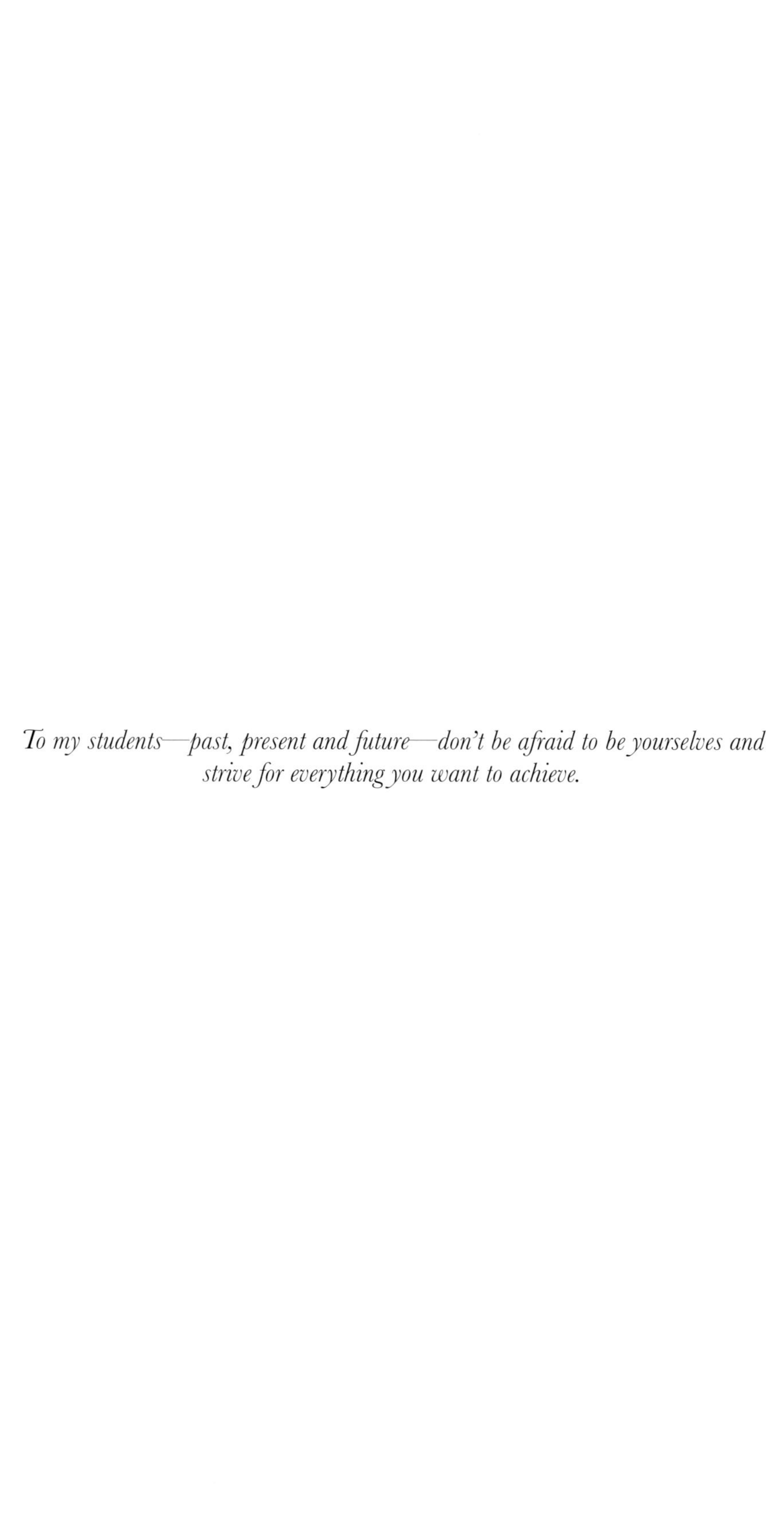

To my students—past, present and future—don't be afraid to be yourselves and strive for everything you want to achieve.

CONTENTS

PREFACE

When I was working through my undergraduate program at The College of Saint Rose, I was introduced to a quote by one of my professors: "History will be kind to me, for I intend to write it." That quote is credited to Winston Churchill and is one that has stuck with me through the years as I learned about the various methods for historical interpretation and writing, the different lenses and philosophies involved in the act and study of history. Often, we hear that "to the victor goes the spoils," and one such spoil is the right to tell the story. Because of this, enthusiasts of history, those who may have only a rudimentary knowledge of history and those who are not specifically trained in history may be learning only half the "story" when it comes to events. It is because of this lack of knowledge that I wanted to focus on stories that have been lost to American history, stories in the era of America's founding that may have been lost to us because they were deemed not relevant, as well as perspectives of people who were there but, because they fought for the "wrong side," have been tucked away in archives, waiting for someone to come along and read them, find them appealing and tell them.

I was inspired to write about the Loyalists, the American colonists who, despite being born in what would become the United States of America, sided with the British during the American Revolution. I wanted an inclusive view of history. As just stated, facts are sometimes left out because they don't fit the narrative that the "victor" is trying to construct.

New York played a pivotal role in the American Revolution, one that is often overshadowed by events and battles in New England and the southern would-be states. As a middle colony, however, New York was important due to valuable natural resources like wood and nutrient-rich farmland, as well as for its numerous large bodies of water, which were used for transportation and trade. New York was home to three major military campaigns, was the launching point for smaller military excursions and, in the later years of the war, was home to numerous raids in the frontier wilderness lands. In lessons on the Revolutionary period, schools tend to focus on events in Massachusetts and other future states. But New York experienced nearly one-third of all of the major battles and skirmishes during the Revolution. Both sides fighting in the war, the British Loyalists and Regulars fighting to maintain the status quo and the rebellious Patriots/Continentals, vied for control of the land and the important waterways—the Hudson River, Lake Champlain, the St. Lawrence River and New York Harbor. Control of the Hudson River was so important to both sides that American commander in chief General George Washington stated that whoever held the Hudson River and New York City held "the safety of America."

New York was a vital middle colony; if the British and Loyalist forces could control New York, they could divide the New England colonies from the Chesapeake colonies and divide the country before it had the chance to get started. If the Americans could secure both New York City and the Hudson River at its source, they would have a major strategic advantage over the British and Loyalist forces.

Americans tend to believe that the majority of people living in colonial New York, and colonial America as a whole, sided with the Patriot cause. They tend to have a very American-centric point of view when it comes to history and to place themselves in high importance. But we can see through the diaries, letters and other writings of the Revolutionary era that this was not the case. The majority of New Yorkers, particularly those who occupied the Adirondack Mountain region and the other wilderness frontier regions of the future state, were either Loyalist or neutral throughout the war. We even see many instances of people who were "turncoats" and would switch sides for various reasons, the main one being which side had their best interests at heart. Still, the war would affect everyone in all regions of New York in some way and would touch the lives of everyone in what would become the United States of America.

As a social historian, it is my belief that everyone's story has the right to be told, so that we may fully understand what happened in a given period. The events of the American Revolution as they unfolded in the mountainous regions of New York are no exception. The people who lived here, regardless of what side they ultimately chose, had a hand in shaping New York and the Adirondack Mountain region into what it is today. Even with the "America first" point of view that is so prevalent in today's society, we find the names of both prominent and long-forgotten British and Loyalist individuals who played roles in New York's Revolutionary War era.

ACKNOWLEDGEMENTS

I would like to thank the following people for the impacts they have had on me as an individual both within and beyond the field of history.

To the amazing history teachers at Hadley-Luzerne Central School, past and present: Mr. Wilson, Mr. Connelley, Mr. Swanson, Mr. Snyder and Mr. Morrison. Thank you all for teaching me and for inspiring me to follow in your footsteps as a teacher.

To the marvelous Dr. Bridgett Williams-Searle, for guiding me, for pushing me when I needed to be pushed, for providing endless words of encouragement and for continuing to be a role model and source of support long after I graduated.

To my professors at Southern New Hampshire University, for encouraging my research and wanting me to succeed.

To my family, for always wanting what is best for me while also allowing me to travel my own path in life and for encouraging me to keep doing what I'm most passionate about.

To my students, for your encouragement and for being my youngest fans.

To my Todd, for his endless love and support and encouragement to boldly go for everything I strive to achieve; for being by my side through the ups and downs; for loving me through my anxieties, insecurities and imposter syndrome; and for being an amazing life partner.

INTRODUCTION

Tucked away in Upstate New York are over 6.1 million acres of protected forest and wetlands known as the Adirondack State Park. This region of New York is broken up into several counties, including the full counties of Warren, Washington, Hamilton, Essex, Oneida and Franklin as well as parts of St. Lawrence, Herkimer and Clinton. Within those counties are 102 present-day towns and a year-round total population of 132,000 residents. Scarcely populated by modern standards, the Adirondack Mountain region was very different during the colonial, Revolutionary and early republican eras.

The people who live in the Adirondack Mountain region of New York are and always have been a distinct breed. They are shaped by the actions and livelihoods of those who came long before them and harbor a vast range of ideals and ideologies passed down from generation to generation. Many of these individuals are descended from the fur traders, hunters, early merchants and land prospectors who sought to use the region for its bountiful resources. Others are descended from the Iroquois Six Nations, which protected the land and called it home. Still others are from a line of soldiers and civilians alike who sought to defend their homes. And there are countless other individuals with varying backgrounds. These are people who understand their individual and shared pasts.

If there was one period that affected the people of the Adirondack Mountain region in the past and continues to have an effect today, it is the era of the American War for Independence. The people of the Adirondack

Vermont, seen from the top of the Bennington Monument.

Mountain region suffered a great deal during that time. Those on all sides of the conflict—Patriot, Loyalist and neutral or apathetic—endured constant fear, hardship, destruction and death as war tore through the mountains and valleys. New York as a whole played a pivotal role in the American Revolution, one that is often overshadowed by the battles and events in other colonies. Over the course of the war, no state would suffer greater losses in both property and population than New York. It was home to three major military campaigns and nearly one-third of all of the major battles and skirmishes of the Revolution, including actions in the Adirondacks.

The American Revolution is described as a civil war by many. Neighbor fought against neighbor and brother fought against brother as differing opinions and ideals swept through the thirteen colonies. In Upstate New York, as elsewhere, we tend to have a very American-centric point of view when it comes to the history of our state and country. In light of this perspective, the goal of this book is twofold. It seeks to highlight the importance of the Adirondack frontier wilderness lands and the small towns in the region that played major roles in the fight for independence that often go overlooked or ignored. The book also seeks to highlight the well-known, little-known and unknown Loyalist individuals who played major roles in maintaining the status quo in the Adirondack Mountain region prior to the end of 1777.

With other wars and conflicts in America's past, historians often describe the motivations and actions of the opposing side. But the actions and motivations of the Loyalists and British (Crown, Parliament, military members and civilians alike) largely go ignored. It is the duty of the historian to tell the full story. Without a comprehensive history, pieces of the puzzle go missing and parts of the story go ignored and can disappear as time continues to move forward.

1

LAWS, TAXES AND UPSTATE NEW YORKERS' RESPONSES

In American history, it is believed that the majority of the colonists were against British rule and wanted to establish a sovereign nation. That couldn't be further from the case in Upstate New York, as many people were Loyalist-leaning or apathetic about the war, believing themselves to be far enough removed from the supposed tyranny and the skirmishes that had broken out elsewhere, such as in Massachusetts, Connecticut, Maryland and the Carolinas. But the shifting laws and taxes affected everyone, and New Yorkers had varying responses to them.

What would become the American War for Independence was a full-scale economic, political and social conflict and was what Patriot-supporting Americans described as a response to harsh colonial laws and taxes at the conclusion of the global Seven Years' War, which had its jumping-off point in the 1750s as French and English colonists fought for control of contested land in North America. The events of that war left the British coffers empty, and the only solution was to levy taxes on the residents of all British-held colonies.

Despite the colonial governors' contact with the lawmakers in Parliament, many of the American colonists claimed that they had no representation when it came to parliamentary procedures and that their voices were not being heard. "No taxation without representation" became a rousing battle cry against king and country.

The British flag flying at Rogers Island Visitor Center in Fort Edward, New York.

Upstate New Yorkers railed against the taxes being levied on them, just as their counterparts in other colonies were doing. Of the numerous acts that Britain passed between 1763 and 1774, those that most affected New Yorkers were the Stamp Act of 1765, the Tea Act of 1773 and the Quartering Act of 1774.

THE STAMP ACT

The Stamp Act of 1765 angered New Yorkers, and others, because it permeated every facet of life. Every paper product—writing paper, maps, playing cards, newspapers, pamphlets, calendars and more—was taxed. Although the Stamp Act was passed by Parliament in March 1765, it did not take effect until November 1, 1765. This gave newspaper printers and others who heavily relied on paper products for their livelihoods time to circumvent the law, allowing for the printing of books, newspapers, broadsides, almanacs and more sans stamps.

The Stamp Act stated, in part:

> *King George III, An Act for granting and applying certain stamp duties, 1765*
>
> *An act for granting and applying certain stamp duties, and other duties, in the British colonies and plantations in America, towards further defraying the expences of defending, protecting, and securing the same; and for amending such parts of the several acts of parliament relating to the trade and revenues of the said colonies and plantations, as direct the manner of determining and recovering the penalties and forfeitures therein mentioned.*
>
> *WHEREAS by an act made in the last session of parliament, several duties were granted, continued, and appropriated, towards defraying the expences of defending, protecting, and securing, the British colonies and plantations in America: and whereas it is just and necessary, that provision be made for raising a further revenue within your Majesty's dominions in America, towards defraying the said expences: we, your Majesty's most dutiful and loyal subjects, the commons of Great Britain in parliament assembled, have therefore resolved to give and grant unto your Majesty the several rates and duties herein after mentioned; and do most humbly beseech your Majesty that it may be enacted, and be it enacted by the King's most excellent majesty, by and with the advice and consent of the lords spiritual and temporal, and commons, in this present parliament assembled, and by the authority of the same, That from and after the first day of November, one thousand seven hundred and sixty five, there shall be raised, levied, collected, and paid unto his Majesty, his heirs, and successors, throughout the colonies and plantations in America which now are, or hereafter may be, under the dominion of his Majesty, his heirs and successors,*
>
> *For every skin or piece of vellum or parchment, or sheet or piece of paper, on which shall be ingrossed, written, or printed, any licence, appointment, or*

(279)

Anno quinto

Georgii III. Regis.

C A P. XII.

An Act for granting and applying certain Stamp Duties, and other Duties, in the *British* Colonies and Plantations in *America*, towards further defraying the Expences of defending, protecting, and securing the same; and for amending such Parts of the several Acts of Parliament relating to the Trade and Revenues of the said Colonies and Plantations, as direct the Manner of determining and recovering the Penalties and Forfeitures therein mentioned.

HEREAS by an Act made in the last Session of Parliament, several Duties were granted, continued, and appropriated, towards defraying the Expences of defending, protecting, and securing, the British Colonies and Plantations in America: And whereas it is just and necessary, that Provision be made for raising a further Revenue within Your Majesty's Dominions in America, towards defraying the said Expences: We, Your Majesty's most dutiful and loyal Subjects, the Commons of Great Britain in Parliament assembled, have Preamble.

4 A 2

5

Image of the Stamp Act pamphlet. Photo credit: The Stamp Act, pamphlet, published in London, 1765. *The Gilder Lehrman Institute, GLC03562.11.*

admission of any counsellor, solicitor, attorney, advocate, or proctor, to practice in any court, or of any notary within the said colonies and plantations, a stamp duty of ten pounds.

For every skin or piece of vellum or parchment, or sheet or piece of paper, on which shall be ingrossed, written, or printed, any note or bill of lading, which shall be signed for any kind of goods, wares, or merchandize, to be exported from…within the said colonies and plantations, a stamp duty of four pence.

For every skin or piece of vellum or parchment, or sheet or piece of paper, on which shall be ingrossed, written, or printed, any licence for retailing of wine, to be granted to any person who shall take out a licence for retailing of spirituous liquors, within the said colonies and plantations, a stamp duty of three pounds.

For every skin or piece of vellum or parchment, or sheet or piece of paper, on which shall be ingrossed, written, or printed, any notarial act, bond, deed, letter, of attorney, procuration, mortgage, release, or other obligatory instrument, not herein before charged, within the said colonies and plantations, a stamp duty of two shillings and three pence.

And for and upon every pack of playing cards, and all dice, which shall be sold or used within the said colonies and plantations, the several stamp duties following (that is to say)

For every pack of such cards, the sum of one shilling.

And for every pair of such dice, the sum of ten shillings.

And for and upon every paper, commonly called a pamphlet, and upon every newspaper, containing publick news, intelligence, or occurrences, which shall be printed, dispersed, and made publick, within any of the said colonies and plantations, and for and upon such advertisements as are herein after mentioned, the respective duties following (that is to say)

For every other almanack or calendar for any one particular year, which shall be written or printed within the said colonies or plantations, a stamp duty of four pence.

Printers would fan the flames of hatred for the Stamp Act by warning the colonists of just how pervasive the new tax would be. With this knowledge, protests broke out in the colonies, including the Stamp Act Riot in New York City. On November 1, 1765, angry New Yorkers took to the streets to protest the act. The protesters burned effigies of colonial Lieutenant Governor Cadwallader Colden and Satan on a gallows before burning the acting governor's carriage in a bonfire and burning the home of the commander of Fort George.

Protests and rioting against the Stamp Act occurred in Albany as well. These protests were led by the Albany Sons of Liberty. As with the New York City protests, once the names for the local stamp tax collector and deputy were chosen—and their names unwisely published in the papers—the Albanians burned effigies and destroyed property, much like their downstate counterparts. The Sons of Liberty were prominent in Albany, and their protests were widespread. As some of the protests turned violent, British soldiers were garrisoned in Albany. If more soldiers were needed, they could be marched up from their garrisons in New York City.

Farther upstate, in the rural Adirondack Mountain region, the people did not have the same response to the Stamp Act as their Capital Region and Downstate counterparts did. The people of the Adirondacks and the western frontier region of New York operated on a bartering system for goods and services, so they were not concerned with the impending collection of the excise tax.

Benjamin Franklin and other delegates could not predict the reaction to the Stamp Act by the general public, but they did warn of the volatile nature of the colonies, under pressure from having won a war over territory they could not expand into as well as a lack of parliamentary representation.

Despite the rioting, Parliament's reaction was calm, and the bicameral legislature decided to wait a few months before repealing the Stamp Act, giving the colonies time to accept the act rather than punish the colonists right away. But Parliament's refusal to back down over the Stamp Act was a move in defense of the law on its own. Had the American colonists not reacted violently against government officials, Parliament may have been willing to compromise with the colonies earlier.

Parliament would repeal the Stamp Act, but more attempts to levy excise taxes on the colonies to refill British coffers were put into place in its stead, including in part the notorious Tea Act.

The Tea Act

Contrary to popular belief, the Tea Act of 1773 was not a tax on tea. The act established the floundering British East India Company as a monopoly, forcing merchants to purchase their stock from the company and eliminating competition and trade with foreign entities. In Boston, the Tea Act of 1773 saw a protest that came to be known as the Boston Tea Party in December 1773.

But Boston was not host to the only tea party in the American colonies. On April 18, 1774, the *Nancy*, commanded by Captain Benjamin Lockyer, landed at Sandy Hook with a cargo of 698 cases of tea from the British East India Company. Lockyer was threatened by the colonists to return to England or lose his life, and local Patriots took control of the ship. The Patriots held the crew and escorted Lockyer into New York City, where he agreed to return to England with the tea and began procuring supplies for the trip. A few days later, on April 22, the ship *London* arrived under the command of a man known only as Captain Chambers. Captain Chambers had claimed that there was no tea aboard the *London*, but the Sons of Liberty received word from Philadelphia that Chambers had 18 chests of tea hidden on the *London* that he was planning to sell for his own profit. Chambers was seized, the ship was searched and the tea was destroyed. Afterward, Captains Lockyer and Chambers left New York to return to England.

The British Parliament responded to the various tea protests by passing the Coercive Acts, also known as the Intolerable Acts, in 1774. Except for the Quartering Act, the Coercive Acts were largely focused on the Massachusetts colony, where local government was limited, and Boston Harbor was closed.

The Quartering Act

Although much of New York, particularly New York City, was Loyalist-leaning, New Yorkers still protested the infamous Quartering Act, particularly in the Albany area. There, colonists experienced the quartering of troops throughout the Seven Years' War. John Campbell, the Earl of Loudoun (for whom Loudounville is named), lamented that the British were unsuccessful in the 1755 campaign due to not having winter quarters near the front lines. Campbell sought to rectify the situation when he assumed command of the

British forces. He urged the colonial governors of New York, Massachusetts and Pennsylvania to construct barracks in Albany, New York City, Boston and Philadelphia. But with funding low, Albany did not see the erection of barracks. Troops moving through the future state capital were instead forcibly housed in privately owned residences under Campbell's command.

The colonists in Albany benefited greatly from the British presence in the small city. Laborers, tavern keepers, inn owners, artisans and merchants lined their pockets while providing goods to their "visitors." The aristocratic families of Dutch and British descent rubbed elbows with British officers. But differences in identity politics would cause strife between the Albany colonists and the British army.

In 1664, Peter Stuyvesant, the last Dutch colonial governor of New Netherland, ceded the territory peacefully to the British. The land was then split into New York and New Jersey. By the time of the Seven Years' War, the New York colonists considered themselves to be Britons. But because the Dutch once controlled the territory and Dutch families (such as the Schuylers, Rensselaers, Ten Broecks and others) were still prominent in the area, the British did not consider the Albany colonists to be Britons. Due to these differences in identity politics, the British army used this non-British view of the Albany colonists to justify their harsh quartering policies.

The British army began quartering troops in Albany in 1756. General James Abercromby quartered his Forty-Second Highland Regiment (more commonly known as the Black Watch) in the city. At first, the Albany colonists seemed pleased to host the troops. But the manner in which some of the soldiers comported themselves, including drunk and disorderly conduct in the city's streets, turned the stomachs of many colonists, who began to view the soldiers as brutes. On a visit to the city by the Earl of Loudoun, some of the colonists brought up their concerns. He initially dismissed the concerns. Like many, the Earl of Loudoun would come to dislike quartering, as he found it unduly taxing to the colonists, who barely had enough space in their homes for their own families, let alone taking in additional people.

Albany was on its way to being a Patriot stronghold in the 1760s due to this forced quartering of troops during what was supposed to be a period of peace. The Albany colonists now had an idea of what close imperial rule would look like if it came to the New York colony. The British army muted the colonists' legal and political voices, British officers interfered with local governments and the increased presence of soldiers brought economic changes to the communities. Even after the Seven Years' War had come to an end, the British army refused to leave the area.

Loyalist forces assembled near Lake George, New York.

The postwar era was prosperous for Albany, as the fur trade was routed through the city, causing an economic and population boom. As a result, the city wanted the British army to return land that the colony had loaned to the army for use during the war. But the army refused. From 1763 through 1767, Albany colonists participated in "riots" that attempted to tear down military buildings on city-owned property. In 1767, the Albany colonists got

Loyalist tents at Lake George Battlefield.

what they asked for, as Major General Thomas Gage ordered the British army to evacuate the city.

The people of Albany primarily sided with the Patriots, because they saw their rights being infringed upon while under occupation. Among their qualms were the following: the quartered troops (British Regulars) did not see the American colonists as British citizens, as they were not born in Great

Britain; there was a lack of political representation in Parliament while taxes were being forced onto the colonists; land the city owned was not being returned for use by the colonists; and other various actions.

Upstate New Yorkers were not quiet in their opinions as they sided with the Patriots, in both words and deeds. Groups such as the Sons of Liberty and the Committee of Public Safety were just as active in Upstate New York as they were in Boston and other New England cities.

Geography, too, would come into play as both the British and Patriots came to realize the importance of New York. The Hudson River, Hudson Valley, Mohawk Valley, Champlain Valley and Lake George region all played prominent roles in the American War for Independence. Patriot-leaning men and women in Upstate New York came from various socioeconomic and racial backgrounds. Men and women alike stood up for what they believed in and fought for freedom from British tyranny.

Loyalist Views

Many textbooks, reflecting an overwhelming Americanist view of history, would have people believe that most colonists sided with the Patriots during the American War for Independence; that men and women who were born in the North American colonies did not side with the British; that the despicable "redcoats" all came from across the pond when Britain was making moves to occupy large cities such as New York City, Boston, Philadelphia and others. But this could not be further from reality. Many New Yorkers, particularly in Upstate New York, chose to side with the British and came to be known as Loyalists, or they attempted to remain neutral, feeling that the war did not directly involve them. They merely wanted to ensure the safety of their families and property and to just exist. Some New York Loyalists did not blindly follow the word of the Crown. Loyalists such as Thomas Jones believed that by remaining loyal to the Crown, he could help perpetuate some of the ideals that the Patriots sought. Jones joined the Continental Congress as a way to discuss the grievances the Patriots had and to find ways to construct a tighter bond with Britain rather than break from it. He believed that the methods the British Crown used (taxation without proper representation in Parliament, a series of harsh laws, etc.) were wrong but that it was better to remain loyal to the Crown and fight the issues through British constitutionalism.

Jones and other Loyalists did not see the Patriots as fighting for their rights, believing instead that their aims could be achieved through means other than a violent uprising. Loyalists believed that Patriots were instead fighting purely to gain power. Other New York Loyalists, such as William Smith, believed similarly to Jones. Smith felt that the Crown had overstepped its role as a mother country by enforcing the laws and taxes that it did, especially without granting proper representation to the North American colonists. But he also believed that the colonists behaved irrationally by jumping to war and feeling that sovereignty was the best option for the people as a whole. Both Jones and Smith believed that war was not the answer, that the North American colonies should remain a vital part of the British Empire, but that the empire should allow for some self-governance. Both men believed that a multi-partisan effort should be made to maintain the empire and that the colonists should have equal representation in Parliament and parliamentary proceedings, as the laws and taxes the Crown was attempting to impose directly affected them. Loyalists like Jones, who scrutinized the Crown yet wanted to remain loyal to it, were met with hostility. In Jones's writings, he described how the Patriots treated the Loyalists, such as being threatened with destruction of property and even death. However, Loyalists were not treated well by British officers and Regulars, either. Having been born and raised in the North American colonies, Loyalists were often seen as "others"—not fully American, as they were choosing to side with the Crown, but not considered fully British, either.

While there were Loyalists like Jones and Smith who did not like the actions of the Crown but did not see splitting from it to be beneficial, other New York Loyalists were staunch supporters of the Crown. Sir William Johnson and his son Sir John Johnson were among them. William Johnson, after fighting in the Seven Years' War at Lake George and constructing Fort William Henry in its vicinity, was able to establish a friendly rapport with the Mohawk of the Hudson Valley and Mohawk Valley regions of New York, and he secured for himself the position of superintendent

Marker for Colonel Edward Jessup in Ontario, Canada. *Photo credit: ontarioplaques.com.*

Above: Jessup's Landing marker in Corinth, New York.

Left: Map of the Jessup Patent. *Photo credit: Adirondack Atlas.*

of Indian Affairs. Through those bonds, many Iroquois individuals, and entire nations, chose to side with the British during the American War for Independence, believing that the British and Loyalists had their best interests in mind. Although Sir William Johnson would pass away in 1774, prior to the outbreak of the Revolutionary War, John Johnson would play a pivotal role. Beginning after 1777, he utilized a combined fighting force of Loyalist soldiers and Iroquois warriors to conduct raids in New York's frontier. Other prominent Loyalists who were either from New York or played important roles in the war's events within its colonial borders were Sir Guy Carleton, Christopher Carleton, Joseph Brant, Walter Butler, John Butler, Edward Jessup and Ebenezer Jessup.

Black Loyalists

From popular media, there is the belief that the majority of the Loyalist and British Regular forces that fought in North America were primarily white, but the American War for Independence would affect people of Amerindian and African descent as well, and they too would take up arms on both sides of the conflict.

In 1775, as the American crisis was reaching a boiling point, John Murray, the Fourth Earl of Dunmore and colonial governor of Virginia, issued a proclamation stating that any slave willing to take up the British cause in the conflict would obtain freedom. Although meant to squash the rebellion in Virginia, Lord Dunmore's proclamation and the formation of Dunmore's Ethiopian Regiment was vital to the British fighting forces in North America, despite being in service only in 1775 and 1776, just as having the Iroquois on their side would be vital to their successes in Upstate New York. In 1779, Sir Henry Clinton, the British commander in chief in North America, issued the Philipsburg Proclamation from the Philipsburg Manor House in Westchester County, New York. This proclamation expanded Dunmore's, stating:

> *Whereas the enemy have adopted a practice of enrolling NEGROES among their Troops, I do hereby give notice That all NEGROES taken in arms, or upon any military Duty, shall be purchased for the public service at a stated Price; the money to be paid to the Captors.*
>
> *But I do most strictly forbid any Person to sell or claim Right over any NEGROE, the property of a Rebel, who may take Refuge with any part*

> *of this Army: And I do promise to every NEGROE who shall desert the Rebel Standard, full security to follow within these Lines, any Occupation which he shall think proper.*
>
> *Given under my Hand, at Head Quarters, PHILIPSBURGH the 30th day of June, 1779.*
>
> *H CLINTON*

Despite the British not treating the Loyalists as equals, they did realize the importance of adding numbers to their forces in North America and even utilized both segregated and integrated regiments throughout the conflict. With the importance of New York as a middle colony, due to the strategic location of previously constructed fortifications and numerous waterways and trade routes, the British realized the value of Loyalist New Yorkers in their ranks, regardless of skin color and position of servitude.

Black men who joined the Loyalist ranks during the war were given myriad tasks. They were utilized for manual labor, such as the construction of breastworks, trenches and other fortifications; as artillerymen; and in civil roles such as quartermasters and engineers, mostly providing logistical support vis-à-vis transportation of food, water, munitions, arms and armaments and maintenance of animals, roads, lodgings and gear used by the frontline troops. They were used in dangerous missions of acquiring intelligence and gathering reinforcements. In such roles, if they were caught, the code of conduct in place at the time restraining the torture of prisoners of war would not apply, as they would be considered runaway slaves. These men also fought in regiments and engaged in battles. Black Loyalists received the opportunity to rise in the ranks, although not to the same extent as their white counterparts. Black Loyalists were awarded officer ranks, both commissioned and noncommissioned, but at lower rates than their white counterparts. They were promised pay, but again, not to the same extent as white soldiers. And at the end of their military service, they were promised freedom if they had entered the service as enslaved men.

Unfortunately, not much is known of the fate of individual Black New York Loyalists during the war itself, but there are sources outlining, at least in part, what happened to many after the war. Following the war, many Black Loyalists sought their freedom in Nova Scotia, Canada; others went overseas to the United Kingdom; and others found themselves in a new settlement in Africa, Sierra Leone, which had been established in the early 1790s.

Although information about the lives of Black New York Loyalists during the War for American Independence is scarce, there is some information about the lives of Black New York Patriots, showing that the war affected everyone regardless of race, sex, socioeconomic status and sociopolitical status.

One such Black Patriot from New York was Benjamin Lattimore. Although not originally from New York (he was born as a free man in Connecticut and relocated to Ulster County some time prior to 1776), he did play a role in the American Revolution as a New Yorker.

At the outbreak of the war, Lattimore was living in New Marbury in Ulster County. In September 1776, he enlisted with the Third New York Regiment of the Continental army. His regiment participated in engagements in New York City in 1776. In 1777, he was stationed at Fort Montgomery in Orange County, New York, when the British captured the fort. Lattimore was then made a servant of British officers but was recaptured by the Americans and sent home.

From the New York State Museum, more of his story unfolds:

> *In 1779, Lattimore sailed with his regiment upriver to Claverack. Blocked by ice, they marched to Albany where they remained for almost two weeks. At that time, he had a glimpse of the community that later would become his home. Marching overland to Schoharie and out the Mohawk Valley, Lattimore was a part of the American offensive to punish the Iroquois for raiding frontier settlements the year before. That summer, he went down Otsego Lake, the Susquehanna River, and then marched all the way to within "hearing the enemy's guns" at Niagara. Lattimore's outfit then returned—destroying a number of Indian settlements and taking part in the Battle of Newtown along the way.…In 1798, Benjamin Lattimore purchased a lot on Plain Street in the first ward. His home at 9 Plain Street was an Albany landmark for the next forty years. In 1803, he extended his holdings through to Hudson Street. In 1811, he purchased another lot above Washington (South Pearl) Street from the estate of General Philip Schuyler.…In 1834, Lattimore applied for a pension as a soldier in the Revolutionary army. His carefully documented and detailed application with supporting documents is on file at the National Archives. For meritorious service, he was allowed a pension of $80 a year and awarded an arrears payment of $240.*

When trying to tell the story of the American Revolution, it's important to look at the war through the eyes of people on both sides of the conflict so that the story is a more complete one.

Portrait of a Black American Revolutionary War sailor by an unknown artist, circa 1780. *Original at the Newport Historical Society.*

IROQUOIS LOYALISTS

During the period between the Seven Years' War and the American War for Independence, the Haudenosaunee, or Six Nations of the Iroquois in New York (the Seneca, Oneida, Onondaga, Cayuga, Mohawk and Tuscarora), attempted to remain neutral as tensions among the American colonists grew. Concerned only with their own place in the New York territory and with what would be in the best interests of their people, individual families and properties, the Iroquois argued among themselves at council meetings before ultimately splitting and choosing sides.

Among the Iroquois, a sort of civil war broke out as nations chose opposing sides in the colonial conflict and as individuals within nations opposed their families and chose differing sides. Iroquois warriors would join the ranks of integrated Loyalist regiments and participate in raiding parties throughout New York and elsewhere.

Two prominent Iroquois Loyalists during this time were Thayendenegea, or Joseph Brant (who was Mohawk), and Cornplanter (Seneca). Both men would lead Iroquois soldiers in battles and raids throughout New York and in other areas in colonial America during the war.

Joseph Brant was the brother-in-law of Sir William Johnson and harbored pro-British tendencies due to the good relations that had been established between the British and the Mohawks prior to and during the Seven Years' War. The threat of revolution would bring a period of instability to the Iroquois, as it would to all in the American colonies that initially attempted to remain neutral until tensions grew to be too much. The Iroquois, as a whole as well as individual nations, wanted to side with those they believed would most benefit the confederacy. For the Mohawks in particular, the British were seen as the right side to ally with. Prior to the outbreak of the Revolution, William Johnson and his son Sir John Johnson befriended the Mohawks in New York and would maintain strong relationships with the nation. Also prior to the outbreak of the Revolution, and as a direct response to the Seven Years' War, the British instituted the Proclamation of 1763 to prevent the further encroachment on lands designated for the various Native American peoples in America. These actions would prompt the Mohawks to take the side of the British during the Revolution, because the Mohawks believed that the British had their best interests in mind, whereas the Patriots disagreed with the validity of the Proclamation of 1763, which would encroach on the land established as Native American territory and thus did not have the best interests of the various Native American tribes in

Left: Mohawk warriors at Fort Ticonderoga.

Below: A statue of Lieutenant Colonel Robert Rogers and five Native Americans in the vicinity of Fort William Henry in Lake George, New York.

Opposite: Camp followers talking on the green.

mind. Chief Joseph Brant took up arms for the British with the outbreak of the war. He led a Loyalist fighting force composed of Mohawk and Seneca warriors. They conducted raids throughout what would become New York State and Pennsylvania. After the surrender of the British at Saratoga in the fall of 1777, Brant's warriors conducted frequent raids around the state beginning in 1778. These raids became known as the Great Burning of the Valleys. For Brant, the loss of the British at Saratoga was a devastating blow, and it was one that meant the Mohawks, Senecas and other Native American nations were in danger. Brant applied to work with Captain John Butler, who then carried out raids in Upstate and Western New York and Pennsylvania with Brant, engaging the Americans in numerous battles.

John Abeel III, more commonly known as Cornplanter, was a Dutch-Seneca war chief during the periods of the Seven Years' War and the American War for Independence. Prior to the outbreak of the Revolution, Cornplanter urged the Iroquois to remain neutral but later decided to join the British, as the majority of the Iroquois had done. During the war, he led attacks on American towns and villages in New York and Pennsylvania. Cornplanter participated in raiding the New York and Pennsylvania borderlands with Joseph Brant and fought against American forces at the Battle of Newtown in present-day Elmira, New York, in 1779 during American general John Sullivan's scorched-earth campaign into the Iroquois ancestral homelands.

Both Brant and Cornplanter became diplomats after the war, negotiating with the new American government as well as the governments of Upper Canada and Great Britain. These treaties and agreements for use of land ensured that their people were taken care of as promised.

LOYALIST WOMEN

Often left out of historical narrative, women played vital, varied roles during the American War for Independence.

Women who sided with the Patriots in New York and in other would-be states tended to be more hands-on than their Loyalist counterparts. Patriot women were more likely to be camp followers, accompanying their husbands, brothers or sons from battle to battle and doing menial work that helped the soldiers (such as laundry, cooking, getting water and more). These female camp followers were the relatives of foot soldiers and high-ranking officers alike. Patriot women also worked as spies, passing along secret messages smuggled in recipes and letters to loved ones and other seemingly innocuous means. And Patriot women helped on the home front by taking care of the shops if they were of the merchant class and of the farms and homesteads, where they produced grains and tended to the barn animals that would be used as meat.

Loyalist women, on the other hand, were less likely to be camp followers, although some were. These women were likely to act as spies while working within the scope of their regular professions, if they had one. For example, some Loyalist women worked as midwives or tended to their family's shop. Other Loyalists, those who could speak English as well as a Native language fluently, were employed by the British and Loyalist military as interpreters.

Two Loyalist women of prominence had roles in the Revolution in Upstate New York: Lady Harriet Acland and Baroness Frederika Charlotte Riedesel.

Lady Harriet Acland (sometimes spelled "Ackland") was the wife of John Dyke Acland, the heir apparent of the seventh baron of Killerton in Somerset, England, and an officer of the Twentieth Regiment of Foot during the War for American Independence. Lady Acland traveled with her husband to North America and followed him to the battlefields where he fought. She was present to witness General John Burgoyne's 1777 surrender to General Horatio Gates at the conclusion of the Saratoga Campaign. Lady Acland was known as a diarist and wrote about her Revolutionary experiences. Using the flowery language of the time, Lady Acland recorded the daily goings-on around her and her feelings toward the war and even wrote a great deal about the battles she witnessed. At the Battle of Bemis Heights, the second battle to have occurred at what is now the Saratoga National Battlefield Park, Lady Acland sought refuge from the fighting with the wounded and infirm while her husband commanded the grenadiers at the most exposed area of the field on that day. Waiting anxiously to hear of the fate of her husband, Lady Acland as well as the wives of two other officers helped treat the wounded soldiers. Unfortunately, Major Acland was injured during the Battle of Bemis Heights and taken prisoner by the Patriots after it was announced that the British had lost the battle. With her husband wounded and captured, Acland wrote to General Burgoyne via his aide-de-camp, saying that she wanted to go to the American side to be with her husband. Reluctantly, Burgoyne let her go. In her diary, Acland recounted the treatment she received while on the Patriot side of the battlefield. When she arrived, she was invited into the guardhouse of Major Henry Dearborn, who made her a cup of tea and informed her that her husband was safe. She spoke with General Gates, who treated her kindly, and she was given an escort to General Enoch Poor's quarters, where her husband was located. She was allowed to stay by his side until he was transferred to Albany. The Patriots who came in contact with Lady Acland noted her loyal devotion to her husband. Major Acland also noted the treatment he received as a British captive and, after he was paroled, advocated for better treatment of captured Patriot soldiers regardless of rank.

Baroness Frederika Charlotte Riedesel was the wife of General Baron Friedrich Adolf Riedesel, who commanded the German Brunswickers during Burgoyne's 1777 campaign. When Friedrich was appointed to his command, the baroness, along with their three children, followed him to North America. Like Lady Acland, the baroness wrote in a diary during the war and recounted her experiences during the Saratoga Campaign. Although considered a woman of rank, as her husband was a commanding officer, the baroness faced hardships throughout the Sarasota Campaign. She noted that the soldiers had little in the way of rations, and she paid the soldiers who were kind and offered her food for her three young children. For the officers, the baroness would throw dinner parties. One such party was to happen on October 7, 1777, with Generals Burgoyne, William Phillips, Simon Fraser and her husband, but battle erupted at Bemis Heights. As the baroness waited for the men to arrive, General Fraser was brought in on a stretcher and placed on the table, having been mortally wounded by a member of Colonel Daniel Morgan's Kentucky Riflemen on the Patriot side. As the battle continued, the baroness was informed that her husband had also been wounded and been taken prisoner by the Patriots after it was announced that the British lost the battle. The baroness waited anxiously for word of her own husband. He was safe, and he called on his wife and children to join him in the Patriot camp, where they dined with British and American generals alike. The Riedesels, like the Aclands, were part of the capitulation on October 17, 1777, as Burgoyne surrendered his army.

WHEN THE WAR FOR American Independence is studied, one question often stands out: "How revolutionary was the American Revolution, and for whom?" This question is one that is only ever asked of the Americans, but the question of how the war affected those who chose to remain loyal to the British Crown should also be asked. If the whole story of the American Revolutionary War is to be told, then the perspectives of those on both sides must be acknowledged, the reasons why sides were chosen must be explained and the military movements of both sides must be examined. So, as the war tore through the colony, as cities were occupied and the frontiersmen of the backcountry were confronted with raids of their fortifications and homesteads, how did those who were apathetic toward the war cope? How did the Loyalists cope? How did the Upstate New Yorkers, specifically those who resided in the untamed wilderness of the Adirondack Mountain region, affect the war? And how were they affected by it?

Women's garments from the Revolutionary era.

2

THE LOYALIST AND REGULAR REGIMENTS IN THE ADIRONDACKS

The British and Loyalist army in North America was extremely well organized. What would become the state of New York had a sizeable Loyalist population, and those men were eager to join the military and take up arms for their king and maintain the status quo for their families. Although the exact number of Loyalists who joined the ranks remains unknown, the different detachments present in Upstate New York, their establishment and the exact role they played are known. In the St. Lawrence, Lake Champlain, Hudson Valley and Mohawk Valley regions, the Loyalist men who joined the ranks were as passionate for their cause as were the men they fought against. Many of them resided in the areas around New York where they found themselves fighting, and they fought with the same fury to protect their families, land and other properties as did their Patriot counterparts. These men were organized in several regiments and detachments across the state. Although the Loyalists lost the war and America gained its independence from Great Britain, Canada grew because of these men, as many settled in Upper Canada and made names for themselves there.

The Twentieth Regiment of Foot

The Twentieth Regiment of Foot, also known as the Lancashire Fusiliers and the Two Tens (due to the use of Roman numerals *XX*) served in the Canadian campaign in 1776 and in General John Burgoyne's 1777 campaign. In the Canadian campaign, the regiment assisted in the relief of Quebec in May 1776. In 1777, it fought until it was taken as part of the capitulation of Burgoyne's army at the conclusion of the Battle of Bemis Heights.

The King's Royal Regiment of New York

In June 1776, after making his escape to avoid arrest by the Americans for his Loyalist leanings, Sir John Johnson raised the King's Royal Regiment of New York, known colloquially as Johnson's Greens. This unit was made up of refugees from the Mohawk and Schoharie Valleys, many also having fled to Canada to escape arrest by the Americans, which was beneficial to the British, who could successfully carry out raids in those upstate areas and ensure that no farmhouse, no matter how remote, was left unmolested. Johnson's Greens would eventually form two battalions and utilize Oswego as its jumping-off point for the raids it led. Johnson was known for his raids throughout his former homeland of Upstate New York and would also cut his teeth on frontier warfare at the Battle of Oriskany during Burgoyne's 1777 campaign. Johnson's Greens would become known—and feared—for the savagery they displayed toward their former neighbors and on any other enemies they encountered.

Sir John Johnson had inherited his father's title. Sir William Johnson was a Scottish fur trader who immigrated to the Mohawk Valley earlier in the eighteenth century and was known for establishing relations with the Six Nations of the Iroquois on behalf of Great Britain at the time of the pivotal Seven Years' War. The title and John's loyalties to Great Britain came with a price—the Americans had threatened Johnson and others with arrest and had begun destroying Loyalist-owned businesses, mills and homes. Johnson went so far as to fortify his home and arm both the white tenants on the Johnson patent and Iroquois allies, who also saw threats from American rebels. Fearing for their lives, many Loyalists in New York fled to Canada.

Around the time many New York Loyalists fled to Canada, the Americans' Continental Congress raised an army and sought to invade Canada. At Quebec, the American forces led by General Richard Montgomery, among others, were defeated in the winter of 1775–76. Although the Americans' invasion of Canada had failed, they were causing distress in the Mohawk Valley and making moves against Johnson's property. Johnson had been warned of the Americans' movements—they had disarmed his tenants and were planning to arrest him. With his tenants defenseless, and with Johnson himself unable to launch a defense of his home, he had no choice but to escape north. With two hundred followers and an unknown number of Mohawk warriors, Johnson made his way to Canada. The escape was long and arduous, as the band had to make its way through the wintry Adirondack Mountains with few weapons and provisions. But in the spring of 1776, Johnson's band, weakened and starving, arrived in Montreal. One of the first things Johnson did on arriving in Montreal was seek out the governor for approval to raise his own regiment, which was granted by Governor Guy Carleton. Johnson began recruiting shortly after the approval. The King's Royal Regiment of New York was composed primarily of those who had followed Johnson to Canada, but many others volunteered for the regiment as well.

The first major campaign that Johnson's Greens participated in was the Battle of Oriskany, a major engagement of Burgoyne's 1777 campaign. While a large British fighting force moved south from Canada to invade New York, another force moved east from Oswego with the intent to overpower the Mohawk Valley. Both of these forces moved as far as the American garrison at Fort Stanwix, where they would make their attack. An American militia of the valley moved to relieve the besieged fort. The British were informed by this movement, and Johnson's Greens, the Indian Department Rangers, Native Americans from the Six Nations and Joseph Brant's forces lay in wait in Oriskany. This ambush devastated the Americans, and their general, Nicholas Herkimer, was fatally wounded in the assault. The Battle of Oriskany was a major victory not only for the British but also for Johnson's Greens, which endured its first military encounter.

Throughout the remainder of the Revolution, Johnson's Greens continued to prove their military strength with a number of raids into their former communities in the Mohawk and Schoharie Valleys. With these raids, Johnson was able to achieve several objectives. His men rescued Loyalists who were forced to endure raids by the Americans; they destroyed local farms, homes, livestock and harvests intended to feed the American military; and lowered the morale of the American military and those with Patriot leanings in the Mohawk and Schoharie Valleys. A major raiding campaign Johnson and his Greens were involved in was called the Burning of the Valleys. This was a 1780 campaign perpetrated by Sir John Johnson and Joseph Brant with the goal of utter destruction. The Burning of the Valleys was so effective on the New York frontier that long after the American Revolution concluded, much of the land of the Mohawk Valley was rendered useless. But with the stroke of a pen, the land that the Loyalists had fought so hard to maintain control of, the land many of them had called home, was granted to the new United States of America.

The Queen's American Rangers

The Queen's American Rangers, named for Queen Charlotte, the wife of King George III, was established in 1776 under the provisional command of Major Robert Rogers. Rogers came to prominence during the Seven Years' War, but during the American War for Independence, his shifting alliances caused suspicion to both the Patriots and the British/Loyalists.

Major Robert Rogers was an interesting character. Born in New Hampshire in 1731, he fought in King George's War as a teenager, guarding the New Hampshire frontier from raids carried out by Native Americans. He served in two scouting parties, under Captain Daniel Ladd and Captain Ebenezer Eastman, where he was trained in guerrilla warfare. In 1755, Rogers was given permission to muster troops in New Hampshire for a light infantry company. Although formally known as the Queen's Rangers, it became colloquially known as Roger's Rangers. They wore green and brown uniforms, very much unlike the standard red British uniform used in colonial North America and elsewhere. The unit used an island in the vicinity of Fort Edward, New York, as training grounds and used the Lake George / Lake Champlain regions as bases of operations.

The original Queen's Rangers disbanded in 1761 after the Seven Years' War, which left Rogers deep in debt, as he had outfitted the rangers (uniforms, provisions, equipment, rations, etc.) using personal funds. His unorthodox guerrilla tactics (at least by British standards at the time) and his twenty-eight rules for ranging are still recognized and utilized by the U.S. Army Rangers. After the Seven Years' War and after many imprisonments and failed attempts to obtain a permanent position with the British government despite his much-earned war status, Rogers offered his services to the Continental Congress. Commander in chief of the Continental army General George Washington was wary of Rogers and denied his request of command. In 1776, Rogers, on the side of the British, was granted a provincial commission as a lieutenant colonel in the British army and was then able to raise troops for his new corps of rangers.

A statue depicting Robert Rogers, along with plaques stating Rogers Rangers Standing Orders.

The Queen's American Rangers was composed of inexperienced rank-and-file soldiers and officers, and the majority of the troops came from Staten Island. This was a Loyalist haven, whereas Manhattan and Long Island were primarily Patriot strongholds (regardless of, or maybe due to, the

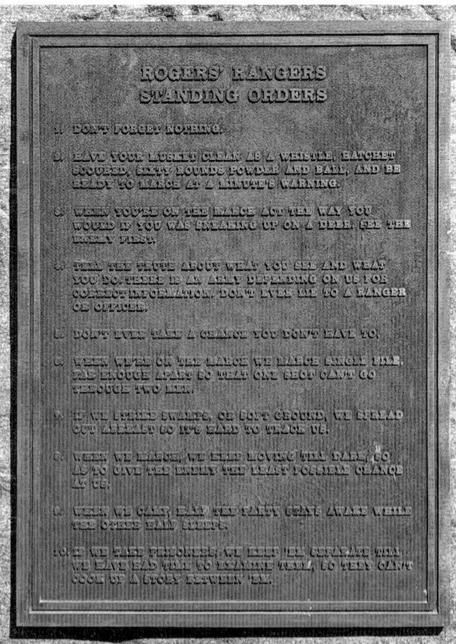

Top, left: A close-up of the plaque on a statue of Robert Rogers.

Top, right: Rogers Rangers standing orders plaque on a statue of Robert Rogers.

Bottom, left: Plaque at the Rogers Island Visitor Center in Fort Edward, New York. The plaque states the former names of Fort Edward and also states that the area was the headquarters of the North American–British Expeditionary Forces.

Bottom, right: A plaque dedicated to the British expeditionary forces at Rogers Island Visitor Center.

The scenery at Rogers Island Visitor Center.

British occupation in New York City). In early 1777, the Queen's American Rangers patrolled Long Island during the Battle of Harlem Heights. This was only the beginning of what the Rangers would do until being formally disbanded in 1783.

Rogers did not serve as a commanding officer of the Queen's American Rangers for the entire duration of the war. In October 1777, John Graves Simcoe was given command of the Rangers, which would then be colloquially known as Simcoe's Rangers. Under Simcoe's command, the Queen's American Rangers was one of the most successful British regiments of the war, seeing action in New York, New Jersey and South Carolina.

The King's American Rangers

The King's American Rangers were mustered in 1779 and officially disbanded in 1794. During the years it was active, the King's Rangers had two battalions, one commanded by Major Robert Rogers and the second commanded by his brother Major Commandant James Rogers. The Rogers siblings recruited the majority of their men from Nova Scotia. Each battalion consisted of ten companies for a total of just over 1,200 rangers.

In July 1779, the King's American Rangers were involved in scouting missions in the vicinity of Fort St. Johns on the Richelieu River, which is

Loyalists having a meeting.

Top: Reenactors loading their muskets.

Bottom: Loyalists mingling on the green.

present-day St. Jean in Quebec. The King's Rangers were also involved in scouting missions in the New York frontier, the Lake Champlain region and into the borderlands that would become Vermont. The King's American Rangers participated in raids against Fort Anne (now known as Fort Ann, as the "e" was later dropped) and the decrepit Fort George on Lake George. They were also instrumental in the 1780 raid on Ball's Town (now Ballston). Members of the King's American Rangers sometimes acted as spies, dressed as civilians, to gather military intelligence against the rebel Patriot forces.

In the 1780s, toward the end of the war, the King's American Rangers took on a number of roles that were both within and outside their regular scope of orders and actions. Majors Robert and James Rogers were given the order by General Frederick Haldimand that the primary tasks for the rangers would be to act as scouts and reconnaissance for other corps, to carry dispatches, to construct fortifications and perform general garrison duties, to assist Loyalist refugees as they made their way to Upper Canada during the later years of the war and during the early years of the new republic, to guard prisoners of war and to be employed as members of the secret service.

The King's Loyal Americans

The King's Loyal Americans was a long-standing military regiment during the American Revolution in Upstate New York. The regiment was originally raised and commanded by Ebenezer Jessup in 1776 but in the 1780s was commanded by his brother Edward. The Jessups had lived in Connecticut for generations, but brothers Edward and Ebenezer moved to the Upper Nine Partners Patent in Dutchess County in the 1740s. Through a series of equitable purchases from Sir William Johnson and from the Mohawks, the Jessup brothers came to own a great deal of property in the Hudson Valley region of Upstate New York. The property they purchased, which would be known as the Jessup Patent, became the towns of Lake Luzerne, Hadley, Corinth (then called Jessup's Landing), Warrensburg, Thurman, Chestertown and Johnsburg. As revolutionary fervor spread, the Jessups had to flee New York for fear of arrest by the Patriots for their loyalty to the Crown. The Jessups took up arms against their Patriot neighbors and enlisted in Burgoyne's army. After the British defeat at Saratoga in

1777, the brothers led raids through the New York frontier for a time. As the war raged on, Ebenezer settled in Canada with his wife and children to keep them out of harm's way, as the Patriots began to arrest Loyalists and punish them by either, or both, confiscating property and killing them under the crime of treason to the United States. Edward, despite the great risks, continued to lead the King's Loyal Americans, known colloquially as "Jessup's Rangers," throughout the remainder of the war.

Ebenezer and Edward Jessup were prosperous Adirondack land barons and came to own much of present-day Warren County. The brothers established several towns and constructed mills and ferries in those towns, providing employment for the people who came to settle in the patent. In the mid-1770s, although the Revolution had not yet been officially declared but the fervor of it spread in the New York frontier, the colonists in the Jessup Patent who had Patriot leanings began to protest the Jessups for being Loyalists, burning down the mills and destroying the ferries. At the threat of arrest and death, the Jessups fled up the Sacandaga River and rendezvoused with Sir John Johnson and other Loyalists also escaping arrest by the Patriots at Fish House, New York, and continued to Canada in the winter of 1775. The summer of 1776 saw the British under Sir Guy Carleton successfully drive American forces out of Quebec after a failed attempt at an invasion. At the end of this event, the Jessups led a group of around eighty Loyalists to join Carleton at Crown Point. This group of Loyalists under the Jessups became attached to Sir John Johnson's regiment, the King's Royal Regiment of New York, or Johnson's Greens.

Throughout the course of the war, but with an increase in the number of raids in 1781 through 1783, Edward Jessup led his rangers throughout the New York frontier and participated in raids led by Joseph Brant and John Johnson, such as General Burgoyne's 1777 campaign, the raid on Ball's Town and raids on towns such as Fort Edward, Fort Ann(e), Queensbury, Kingsbury and Glens Falls. As the war drew to an end and as hostilities between the British army and the American army eased, Jessup's Rangers were ordered to disband in December 1783. Both of the Jessups petitioned to regain their land in New York, but to no avail. They lived out the rest of their days in Canada, where they established villages along the St. Lawrence River.

The Queen's Loyal Rangers

The Queen's Loyal Rangers, under the command of John Peters from Connecticut, accompanied Burgoyne on his 1777 expedition. In the later war years, beginning in the fall of 1781, the Queen's Loyal Rangers combined with Jessup's King's Loyal Americans and McAlpin's Corps of American Volunteers to form a new corps, the Loyal Rangers. The Queen's Loyal Rangers saw action in a number of battles, including the 1777 British capture of Fort Ticonderoga, the Battle of Hubbardton, the Battle of Bennington and the Battle of Saratoga, and in various small raids throughout the New York frontier.

McAlpin's Corps of American Volunteers

Much like John Peters's Queen's Loyal Rangers, Major Daniel McAlpin's Corps of American Volunteers was originally mustered into action to take part in General Burgoyne's 1777 campaign. The founding of McAlpin's Corps was authorized by Sir William Howe, and the soldiers for the corps were recruited in the Albany region. McAlpin's Corps participated in a series of battles and raids, but as the war went on, the corps was combined with Peters's Queen's Loyal Rangers and Jessup's King's Loyal Americans in 1781.

At the time that McAlpin's Corps was mustered into action on August 1, 1777, Daniel McAlpin was an elderly British army captain who had retired from service in the Sixtieth Royal American Regiment. He had become a well-to-do landowner in Stillwater, New York, who was harassed by the Patriots for his Loyalist leanings, as others had been. But instead of fleeing to Canada as a majority of Loyalists had done, McAlpin received a warrant from Sir William Howe in the fall of 1776 to raise a Loyalist corps and was recruiting Loyalists to fill its ranks in secret. McAlpin was arrested by the Patriots but was able to escape and went into hiding. In the summer of 1777, when General Burgoyne marched through New York in his famous Saratoga Campaign, McAlpin joined him in July at Fort Edward, New York. The men of McAlpin's Corps of American Volunteers were largely employed in the defense of supply lines during Burgoyne's Saratoga Campaign, but after the British loss at the Battle of Saratoga, many of the 184 men and officers were drafted into other British regiments for the purpose of helping offset

Loyalist officers talking in a group.

the heavy loss of life suffered by the British. Others were entrusted with ensuring that the British pay chest escaped Upstate New York and made it to Canada unmolested by the Patriots prior to Burgoyne's surrender at the heights of Saratoga. But 50 or so of these men were taken prisoner at the time of the British retreat. Despite that, the pay chest was successfully delivered to Canada.

That would not be the end of the corps, though. After the British made their way to Canada after Burgoyne's failure at Saratoga, McAlpin's Corps was assembled into a battalion under the command of Sir John Johnson, combining the corps with his King's Royal Regiment of New York. Command of the new battalion was handed over to McAlpin in May 1779 along with the rank of major commandant. Initially, this new battalion was engaged in building garrisons and fortifications to secure Quebec against another Patriot invasion. Later that year, Major Commandant McAlpin fell ill but continued with his duties until his death in the summer of 1780. At McAlpin's death, control of the corps was granted to Major John Nairne of the Royal Highland Emigrants, but despite the change in command, the battalion was still referred to as McAlpin's Corps of American Volunteers. In the fall of 1781, command of the corps changed hands again. The Corps of American Volunteers, the King's Loyal Americans and the Queen's Loyal Rangers were combined into the Loyal Rangers under the command of Major Edward Jessup.

Now under Edward Jessup, the Loyal Rangers took part in a series of raids in the New York frontier, burning villages and hamlets and destroying crops and livestock so the Patriots could not use those provisions and housings. After the conclusion of the American Revolution, the Loyal Rangers disbanded and resettled in the Canadian province of Ontario, forming the towns of Ernestown, Edwardsburgh, Augustus and Elizabethtown.

The Eighty-Fourth Regiment of Foot

In the early 1770s, prior to the outbreak of the American War for Independence, Sir William Johnson encouraged Irish and Scottish immigrants to settle on the land he had purchased from the Mohawks. Johnson did this as a tactic, as a way to "balance the scales," as those in neighboring patents, primarily Palatine Germans, sided with the Patriots in the impending war. In 1775, the formation of the Eighty-Fourth Regiment of Foot, also known as the Royal Highland Emigrants, was underway, and the corps, under the command of Colonel Allan Maclean, recruited from these men living on Johnson's land as well as men from Nova Scotia, New Brunswick and the Carolinas. Many of the men recruited into this corps were veterans of other corps in previous colonial conflicts. Also in 1775, as Maclean was recruiting for the Eighty-Fourth Regiment of Foot, Major John Small was also recruiting for a corps of loyal Scots, called the Young Royal Highlanders. Major Small's corps became the second battalion of the Royal Highland Emigrants.

The first battalion of the Eighty-Fourth Regiment primarily served in the northern theater of the war, being assigned to defend Fort St. Johns and Quebec, and also as a raiding force within New York's frontier.

British regulars in Stony Creek, New York.

The second battalion of the Eighty-Fourth primarily served in Nova Scotia, where it performed amphibious duties along the coasts of Maine, Georgia, the Carolinas and in Jamaica.

During the War for American Independence, these corps saw both successes and failures in attempting to maintain the status quo in the colonies. To many, these men would be enemies; to others, they were keepers of the peace with the goal to protect their lands, homes and families. The Loyalists who joined the British war effort in the Revolution's later years fought against old neighbors and friends to keep the thirteen colonies intact, and it was these men who would later come to settle in Canada and grow its population.

3
THE KING'S LOYAL NATIVES IN THE ADIRONDACKS

The Loyalist forces in the Adirondack Mountain region in New York were often accompanied by Iroquois warriors in skirmishes, battles and raids.

The Haudenosaunee, or "People of the Longhouse," as the Iroquois called themselves, were a powerful Native American confederacy. Once known as the Five Nations, in 1722, the Iroquois Confederacy accepted the Tuscarora into the fold, and the confederacy became the Six Nations. The Six Nations of the Iroquois was composed of the Mohawk, Onondaga, Oneida, Cayuga, Seneca and Tuscarora peoples.

The Iroquois began building a lasting relationship with the British in the 1750s, as both Britain and France worked to gain the Six Nations as allies in the Seven Years' War. While the French had some initial success with the Senecas, the Six Nations ultimately sided with the British. If a single man could be credited with the alliance, it would be Sir William Johnson. Johnson would become the superintendent of Indian Affairs and would spend his life working to maintain the British-Iroquois relationship. This relationship led to the British victory at the conclusion of the Seven Years' War.

The peace that came with the conclusion of the Seven Years' War was short-lived, as the colonists began pushing farther into Native lands. Six Nations and British colonial leaders met at Fort Stanwix in 1768 to discuss a firm boundary line between the British American colonies and Native land. The treaty would do little to quell the colonists from pushing into Native territories, believing that they had fought for the land in the Seven Years'

Portrait of Sir William Johnson on display at Fort William Henry.

War and that their victory meant they had a right to it. With the staggering costs of the war and the Crown raising taxes and implementing new laws for the colonists to follow, along with the inability to reside on the land they had fought for during the previous armed conflict, a growing rift was formed between the American colonists and the British Crown, and the Natives, particularly the Six Nations, would be drawn into another war.

The Six Nations was not initially drawn into the conflict that would become the Revolutionary War. In fact, the Six Nations did not understand why the colonists were fighting among themselves and had little interest in being drawn into what it saw as a civil war. In the early days of the Revolution, however, leaders of the Oneida Nation declared their neutrality in the war by sending a message to the New York governor. Whether the Crown or the colonies sought their aid, the Oneida would refuse to help. But the course of neutrality chosen by the Six Nations could not be maintained for long, and the Six Nations, and individuals therein, would be forced to choose sides. The majority of the Six Nations, with the exception of the Oneida and the Tuscarora, chose to ally themselves with the British. Their reasons included keeping in line with the old alliance system and believing that their landholdings would be better protected if they sided with the British and the British won.

The Iroquois played monumental roles in the American Revolution, particularly in New York. The Mohawk, specifically, were vital in the British campaign in the future state. Two notable Mohawks who played important roles at this time were siblings Joseph and Molly Brant. Joseph Brant led numerous raids on New York's frontier settlements throughout the war, and his sister was host to various war conferences at Johnson Hall.

MOHAWK

During the American Revolution, most of the Mohawks lived along the Mohawk River in New York, in such places as Canajoharie, Schoharie and Fort Hunter. The Mohawk were among four of the six Iroquois nations to side with the British during the war. They had a longstanding trading relationship with the British and hoped that siding with the British would bring an end to the colonists encroaching on their land in the Mohawk River valley. Joseph acted as a war chief and led successful raids against the localities that supported the Patriots.

Although the Mohawks were known as supporters of the British, a few prominent Mohawk leaders, such as the sachem Tyorhansera, remained neutral throughout the war. Other prominent Mohawk leaders, such as Joseph Louis Cook, a veteran of the Seven Years' War, offered their services to the Americans.

ONEIDA

The Oneida played a major role in the American Revolution, siding with the Patriots against the British. Although the Oneida Nation initially declared its neutrality in what it deemed a civil war, Oneida warriors later fought in several key battles in the Revolution, including at Oriskany and Saratoga. Due to their alliance with the Americans during the Revolution, the Oneida became known as America's first allies.

The Oneida were able to provide the most physical support during the war, especially from 1777 to 1778. They were present at the Battle of

Oriskany during the Saratoga Campaign prior to the start of frontier raids across Upstate and Western New York. The Oneida even provided warriors to General Horatio Gates and General George Washington, with some warriors even staying at Valley Forge in the winter of 1778.

The primary role of the Oneida to the Americans during the war were as scouts, guides and couriers. These were largely support roles but were nonetheless important, as they allowed the Americans to gain intelligence on British military movements and receive aid from nearby regiments. Along with these roles, the Oneida were engaged in scouting expeditions to Oswego and engaged in raids against the Iroquois nations that sided with the British.

Maybe surprisingly, the Oneida were reluctant participants in the Sullivan-Clinton Expedition of 1779 against the Iroquois. The Oneida also provided scouts to counter the British raids in the Hudson and Mohawk Valleys.

Toward the end of the Revolution, the Oneida had lost a great deal due to their decision to side with the Americans. One of their villages had been destroyed, and the nation had to move to the areas of Oriskany and Schenectady for safety. By 1780, some of the surviving Oneida had been forced to change their allegiance and side with the British in order to protect themselves and their families. By the end of the fighting in 1783, people of the Oneida Nation had lost their homes, any wealth they possessed and their overall way of life. They had few resources to fall back on, and it was not until the 1790s that the Oneida received any recompense for their service to the Americans in the war. Between the Oneida and the Tuscarora, the U.S. government paid out around $5,000 to cover the destruction of the homes and crops of its Native American allies.

Onondaga

In the American Revolution, the Onondaga were initially neutral. But, as other Natives had done, individual Onondaga warriors participated in raids against the Americans and their settlements in the New York frontier. The Onondaga as a whole pulled out of its pact of neutrality after the Americans attacked its main villages in April 1779, and the nation sided with the British for the remainder of the war.

At the conclusion of the Revolution, with the American victory, many Onondaga followed Joseph Brant and his Mohawks to Upper Canada, where the Crown gave them land for their loyalty in the war.

Cayuga

The Cayuga were caught in the middle of the Revolution in New York, with some fighting for the British and some for the Americans. Others chose to remain neutral. But the Cayuga, above all, were loyal to their families and to their land, and as both the Americans and the British encroached on their land, the Cayuga defended themselves.

In 1779, General George Washington commissioned Generals John Sullivan and James Clinton to destroy Iroquois villages in Western New York. The Cayuga were heavily affected, as their homes and crops were destroyed. After the war, many individual Cayuga relocated to Ohio and/or Canada, but those who remained negotiated the Treaty of Canadaigua in the 1790s with the United States, which provided for the sovereignty of the Six Nations and established the reach of the federal government over New York State.

Seneca

When the American Revolution broke out, the Seneca initially attempted to remain neutral, as had the other Iroquois nations. But both sides attempted to bring the Seneca into the action. At the Battle of Oriskany, when the Americans defeated the British at Fort Stanwix, they had killed many Seneca warriors and onlookers alike. This event, along with the anti–Native American rhetoric of the Americans, pushed the Seneca to side with the British.

The Seneca and the other Iroquois nations that sided with the British were involved in numerous notable battles and raids in the New York frontier. Although the Seneca and the Iroquois as a whole were active participants in the Revolution, prominent leaders such as Cornplanter and Blacksnake were disgusted by the brutality of the war and the mental toll of having killed so many people. They spoke out against their own actions.

The Seneca suffered at the hands of the Americans during the notorious Sullivan Expedition. After the expedition, the Seneca and other warriors renewed their raids on American settlements in New York as well as on Oneida and Tuscarora settlements, even continuing these raids after the British surrendered at Yorktown. The warriors stopped fighting in 1782 pending the peace negotiations between the British and Americans.

At the conclusion of the war, the Seneca and other Iroquois nations were required to cede all of their lands in New York, just as the British were required to cede their territories in the thirteen colonies to the new United States.

Tuscarora

The entrance of the Tuscarora into the American Revolution was the product of a unique set of circumstances. The Tuscarora, unlike the other five Iroquois nations, were not originally from New York. Prior to 1713, the Tuscarora had inhabited the Carolinas but fled for New York after an event that came to be called the Tuscarora War in order to join the Iroquois Confederacy.

It is difficult to find information about the actions the Tuscarora Nation took during the American Revolution. But there is an abundance of information about the monetary and proprietary claims made by Tuscarora individuals in the wake of the war. According to a document discovered by historian Lyman Draper, who interviewed individuals about the American Revolution in the 1800s, only eight Tuscarora individuals/families claimed losses at the conclusion of the war; several other claimants were members of the Oneida Nation. The document not only lists the claimed losses but also includes accounts describing how these individuals lived during the war. Most of the claimants lost horses and/or other livestock and at least one house. Others, however, claimed more items, highlighting that the area in which they lived had been burned during a raid at this time. Oneida and Tuscarora individuals also attempted to make fraudulent claims, stating that belongings had been destroyed or taken. It was later determined that these individuals were not in the location where they supposedly lost their belongings.

The Tuscarora had sided with the Americans during the Revolution. Of those who played a role in the Continental army, some served as warriors; others served as intelligence gatherers, collecting information on British movements with their own warriors. One prominent Tuscarora Native was Nicholas Cusick. He served in the Revolution for a total of five years, gathering intelligence on enemy Indian groups and their movements for the Americans. Along with a man named Johannas Oosterhout Jr., Cusick submitted a detailed and lengthy report to the New York Council of Safety in August 1777.

The American Revolution destroyed the once great power of the Six Nations. During the war, as a response to four of the six nations siding with the British and for raids they participated in with the British, commander in chief of the Continental army General George Washington sent an expeditionary force under Generals John Sullivan and James Clinton into Central and Western New York with the sole purpose of destroying enemy Iroquois property at Unadilla and Onaquaga. After the Revolution, many of the remaining Iroquois settled in Canada, as many remaining Loyalists did as well. The participation of the Iroquois was tantamount to the success or failure of the raids and of the war in its entirety. The need to delineate among the Six Nations and their reasons for choosing the sides they did is imperative to understanding the remainder of this narrative. The actions taken by the Iroquois during the American Revolution helped shape the course of the war in New York. The four nations that sided with the British were able to successfully assist in battles and carry out raids across New York after the 1777 campaign ended, but their actions were not without consequences.

4
THE ST. LAWRENCE / THOUSAND ISLAND SEAWAY REGION

The St. Lawrence / Thousand Island Seaway region, known today for the St. Lawrence Islands National Park, lies in a very strategic location, in the Frontenac Axis connecting Ontario's Algonquin Provincial Park and New York's Adirondack State Park. The Thousand Island Seaway is known for the more than one thousand islands that dot the area, the product of scraped sediment as glaciers retreated after the Ice Age ten thousand years ago, leaving behind a chain of granite that would form into the islands. The St. Lawrence / Thousand Island Seaway region was home to the Iroquois as well as to the Mississauga Anishinaabe. In the early 1600s, with French (and later English) exploration and colonization, explorers, fur traders and missionaries relied on the location of the islands for movement of goods and people. The region played a role in the Revolutionary War as the Americans attempted to invade Canada in 1775.

The Quebec Act of 1774

Prior to the outbreak of the American War for Independence, the British Parliament placed a series of laws on all of its colonies. One of these laws, the Quebec Act of 1774, was specific to Upper Canada. The act had the goal of reforming Canadian governance in three areas: religion, land claims and overall government power structure.

The St. Lawrence River, with Montreal in the background in the top image.

At the conclusion of the Seven Years' War in 1763, France ceded Quebec and all of its claims in the Ohio Valley to the British. In the Proclamation of 1763, Britain established its colonial policy toward Quebec, which provided for a royal colonial governor and an oath of loyalty that prevented Roman Catholics from serving in Quebec's colonial administration. In 1774, Parliament passed the Quebec Act, which granted emancipation and religious freedom to the Catholic, French-speaking settlers of the Province of Quebec. The act repealed the oath of loyalty and reinstated French civil law alongside British criminal law.

The Americans saw the Quebec Act as one of the "intolerable acts," which would bring them to the brink of war. The Americans, who settled in the thirteen colonies, and some who had begun to settle in Quebec and other areas of Canada, were largely Protestant and held anti-Catholic sentiments. They saw the move to allow Catholics to practice their religion and to serve in colonial administration as an overreach by the British, as if the Crown was establishing a religion in an area, rather than as the reinstatement of religious freedom. The Quebec Act also allowed for the collecting of tithes and allowed Jesuit priests to carry out missions. The Americans saw the religious reforms in the Quebec Act as a threat, believing that the Crown would meddle in their own religious policies. Catholics in Upper Canada were overjoyed by the religious reforms in the act, as they could openly practice their faith and participate in their government without having to give up their religion.

The Quebec Act did not focus only on religious reforms. It also touched on land claims. The act expanded Canada's borders into western American territories. The Americans were angered over this, as an increase in Canadian territory meant a decrease in their own land. Many Americans saw the redistribution of land in Canada as a threat to American expansion. Also, the British in both Great Britain and Canada practiced a system of hereditary nobility, which the Americans despised, when it came to land grants. Money, title or both could earn someone large swaths of land. The land that was being granted to these monied Canadians was land granted to Britain after the end of the Seven Years' War, land that Americans were barred from moving into (the Ohio Valley, which they fought hard to obtain access to during the war).

Finally, the Quebec Act established how the Canadian provincial civil government was to be run. According to the act, the head of the Canadian government was to be appointed by the Crown, and there were no provisions put in place for a democratic government to spring up and flourish. The provincial government was to be autocratic and offer no representation to its people.

The reforms in the Quebec Act of 1774 horrified the Americans, and they believed that they would be able to rally the Canadians to their side during the American War for Independence. But that was not the case, as many Canadians joined the British and Loyalist forces. The Americans believed that since the Canadians had been under British control only since 1760, they would flock to join the Patriot ranks. In reality, the Canadians did not see what they were enduring under British rule as similar to what their American counterparts were experiencing. Many Canadians benefited from

Left: Mary, Queen of the World Cathedral in Montreal, Quebec.

Right: A nun bringing Catholicism to the Native peoples of Montreal.

the Quebec Act. To them, it allowed religious freedom, land ownership and expansion and a government that cared about their well-being despite the lack of a representative branch. Where American colonists in different would-be states struggled to comprehend what was occurring in other areas and labored to form a national identity because of it, the same thing was happening with American-Canadian relations at the time. In 1775, the Americans launched an invasion of Canada to attempt to take control of Quebec and Montreal.

St. Mary and Jesus draped with a rosary.

THE QUEBEC CAMPAIGN

In 1775, the Americans set out to take control of Upper Canada. Their rationale for doing so was twofold. First, the primarily Protestant British colonists had spent over a century locked in imperial warfare with French Catholics over North American territory and viewed Quebec as a threat to both the physical and cultural security of the new nation they were attempting to secure and build. Second, despite the perceived threats to American security, the Americans also viewed Quebec as having commonalities with them, due to the varied backgrounds of its residents, and the Americans wanted the Province of Quebec to have a place in the new American nation. Although this twofold rationale is definitely antipathetic, the Continental Congress felt strongly about bringing Upper Canada into the fold of its new nation, whether the Quebecois wanted to be a part of it or not, and from August 1775 to July 1776, the Americans invaded Canada in the Quebec Campaign.

The Quebec Campaign and the Canadian invasion had four main phases.

The first phase began on August 25, 1775, when American general Richard Montgomery ordered 1,200 men to muster at the recently acquired Fort Ticonderoga to march into the Quebecois territory, where they encamped on the Richelieu River. On September 17, Montgomery's forces moved on to attack Fort St. John's at the northern end of Lake Champlain, where they gained access to Quebec and were able to lay siege to the city. Sir Guy

Carleton, the colonial governor of Quebec, was unable to break the siege by October 30, and his garrison chose to surrender peacefully to the Americans on November 3. From the successful siege of Quebec, Montgomery set his sights on Montreal and surrounded the city. Carleton was unable to defend the city, ordered it to be abandoned and surrendered Montreal without resistance on November 13.

The second phase of the invasion was also underway at this time. The commander in chief of the Continental army, General George Washington, ordered a force of 1,100 men under the command of Colonel Benedict Arnold to proceed to flank Quebec City. Arnold's forces boarded ships in Massachusetts on September 15, sailed up the Atlantic coast to Maine, marched four hundred miles through largely uninhabited wilderness and reached the gates of Quebec City on November 14. As a result of a large number of deaths and desertions, Arnold's men numbered only about 600 when they arrived and awaited reinforcements from Montgomery, which came to them on December 2. The 2 men planned out the siege of Quebec, which they began to carry out in earnest a few days later, on December 5.

The third phase of the campaign was the attack on Quebec, which took place on December 31. Montgomery planned the attack on the city to be a multipronged one against the surrounding fortifications. Troops under Montgomery, Arnold and Colonel James Livingston approached Quebec City while under the cover of a harsh winter snowstorm. The storm turned out to do more harm than good for the Americans, as the Patriot troops were snow-blinded, and their weapons were clogged and did not function properly. The American assault on Quebec City ended with Arnold wounded, Montgomery dead and four hundred Patriot soldiers captured by Loyalist and Quebecois forces. Despite the American defeat and General Montgomery's death, Arnold took over command of the Patriot forces around Quebec City and continued the siege for several more months.

The fourth phase of the Quebec Campaign occurred in May 1776, when the Loyalist and Quebecois forces in Quebec City were reinforced by General John Burgoyne's troops. With Burgoyne's reinforcements, Carleton was able to drive Arnold's forces to retreat toward Upstate New York, where they would eventually be expelled from the Province of Quebec.

The Quebec Campaign was wholly unsuccessful, despite reinforcements of both manpower and cannons from General Philip Schuyler in the early days of the siege, as well as early successes by the Americans in capturing some of the province's smaller fortifications, such as Fort Chambly. An

A French soldier on display at Fort William Henry.

interesting note is that one of the prisoners of war taken by the Americans at the capture of Fort Chambly was Major John André, who was later paroled and earned notoriety in 1780 for his part in Benedict Arnold's treason against the Americans.

Also important to note is that despite many Canadians siding with the British and Loyalists, most participated in "benevolent neutrality" and supported both sides during the Quebec Campaign, providing rations and lodgings to soldiers so they would not starve or freeze in the harsh winter months. Other Canadians, including Indigenous peoples, did sign up to fight on the side of the Americans. These acts—fighting for one side or the other and choosing to remain neutral—show that it was not just the American colonies that were fractured at this time. Other British territories were in turmoil as well.

Perhaps due to the treatment that both the British Loyalists and Americans received during the Canadian campaign, many Loyalists went on to settle in Upper Canada after the American victory in 1781 and the war's official end in 1783.

FORT HALDIMAND AND CARLETON ISLAND

Carleton Island, formerly known as Deer Island, is located in U.S. waters in the south channel of the St. Lawrence River. The island lies about seven miles from Lake Ontario to the west and about three miles from the village of Cape Vincent, New York, to the east. Comprising less than 1,300 acres of land, the island has no sociopolitical significance to either Canada or the United States, but in the era of the American War for Independence, a fort that did play a major role in the war was situated on the island.

Prior to the outbreak of the war, Deer Island was used as a sort of waypoint by British merchants. Large vessels that had no problem navigating Lake Ontario were not fit to sail down the St. Lawrence River. Goods would be deposited on Deer Island, where they were then transferred to smaller vessels.

In the summer of 1777, British general Barrimore St. Leger used Deer Island as a staging ground for the western prong of Burgoyne's campaign. St. Leger also utilized the island in his army's retreat after the siege of Fort Stanwix at the Battle of Oriskany didn't quite go as planned for the British and Loyalist troops.

The British and Loyalist defeat in the 1777 campaign marked the first major British loss of the American Revolution. As a result of this defeat, the British lost access to the Mohawk and Hudson Valleys and to their supply routes.

In need of a new supply route and of a jumping-off point for a series of raids in the New York frontier, the British and Loyalist forces looked to the St. Lawrence / Thousand Island Seaway region.

In 1778, Governor General of Canada Frederick Haldimand instructed the Royal Corps of Engineers to select a site at the eastern end of Lake Ontario to serve a role in the new supply route. Lieutenant William Twiss of the Royal Corps of Engineers, along with John Schank of the British

Royal Navy, scouted the abandoned forts at Cataraqui and Deer Island and selected Deer Island.

Twiss and Schank renamed the island after Sir Guy Carleton, the governor of Quebec. They then outlined the design of the docks, shipways, hospital, fortification, barracks and earthworks. The two men named the fortifications after Haldimand and left the men of the Royal Corps of Engineers to oversee the actual construction.

Although little known, Fort Haldimand and Carleton Island continued to play a prominent role in the Revolution's later years. Fort Haldimand served as a military staging area for the Loyalist raids into the Mohawk and Hudson Valleys, which began in 1778.

Fort Haldimand and Carleton Island also served as the headquarters for naval operations on Lake Ontario and the Upper St. Lawrence River, where the shipyard maintained the Lake Ontario fleet. That is not where the prominence of the fort and the island end, however.

By 1782, as major hostilities were dying down, the entire west end of Carleton Island was occupied by merchants, sailors, soldiers, camp followers, Native Americans and displaced Loyalists. In 1783, after the signing of the Treaty of Paris, the British and Loyalist forces used the island as a waypoint to relocate Loyalist individuals and families who sought resettlement in Upper Canada after having been dispossessed of their landholdings in various Upstate and Western New York areas. Important to note is that, during this time, Cataraqui was renamed Kingston.

British occupation of Carleton Island slowly declined until the island was ceded to the United States in the Jay Treaty of 1796. Despite that, Britain still held the island at the outbreak of the War of 1812, and it officially exchanged hands at the war's end.

The St. Lawrence / Thousand Island Seaway region of New York and Canada played a small role in the American Revolution. The people primarily sided with the British, which allowed for an increase in Loyalist troops who knew the area where they would be fighting. The fact of their being from the area permitted them to remain in Upper Canada after the war came to an end. Also, the land itself was vital, as British and Loyalist troops were able to move cannons, arms, armaments and troops through the area and garrison them at the forts. After the war, the seaway region was used as a jumping-off point for the troops to evacuate Loyalist civilians to their new home in Upper Canada.

5
THE LAKE CHAMPLAIN REGION

Geographically, the Lake Champlain region was the northernmost region within New York's colonial borderlands to see a number of military actions.

After the signing of the Treaty of Paris in 1763, bringing an end to the Seven Years' War, increased British rule came to New York and the other North American colonies. This rule brought increased taxes, a limitation of rights and an increase in the enforcement of trade duties. The colonists viewed these actions by an absentee government as tyranny.

The Lake Champlain region of Upstate New York was a critical strategic arena during the Seven Years' War. Its forts, Fort Ticonderoga and Crown Point, played important roles during the war and would see action again during the American War for Independence, changing hands a number of times over the course of the conflict.

Seizing Arms

Tensions rose in the American colonies after the Boston and New York Tea Parties, even though the various acts and taxes that the British attempted to levy on their colonies had been dropped. The British underestimated the attitudes their American counterparts would have toward the taxes and the quartering of troops in their cities. Letters and arguments in Parliament and the colonial houses of government were not enough to convince the American colonists to remain a part of the British Empire.

Many of the colonists decided to take matters into their own hands by preparing to fight if a break in the relationship between empire and colony came to war. To do this, the Americans began stockpiling arms and ammunition in locations such as Concord, Massachusetts, which was near Boston. British regulars were ferried from Boston to the Charlestown shore with instructions to capture Samuel Adams and John Hancock for inciting revolutionary unrest in the city of Boston as well as to confiscate any arms and ammunition the colonists might be stockpiling and hiding. Following their orders, the regulars prepared to move on Concord, having received intelligence that the American colonists had stockpiled weapons there. In a letter to British general Thomas Gage, a Lieutenant Colonel Smith with the Tenth Regiment of Foot described the action at what is known as the Battles of Lexington and Concord:

> *Lieut. Col. Smith to Governor Gage Boston, April 22, 1775.*
> *Sir, In obedience to your Excellency's commands, I marched on the evening of the 18th inst. with the corps of grenadiers and light infantry for Concord, to execute your Excellency's orders with respect to destroying all ammunition, artillery, tents, &c., collected there, which was effected, having knocked off the trunnions of three pieces of iron ordnance, some new gun carriages, a great number of carriage wheels burnt, a considerable quantity of flour, some gunpowder and musket balls, with other small articles thrown into the river. Notwithstanding we marched with the utmost expedition and secrecy, we found the country had intelligence or strong suspicion of our coming, and fired many signal guns, and rung the alarm bells repeatedly; and were informed, when at Concord, that some cannon had been taken out of the town that day, that others, with some stores, had been carried three days before....*
>
> *I think it proper to observe, that when I had got some miles on the march from Boston, I detached six light infantry companies to march with all expedition to seize the two bridges on different roads beyond Concord. On these companies' arrival at Lexington, I understand, from the report of Major Pitcairn, who was with them, and from many officers, that they found on a green close to the road a body of the country people drawn up in military order, with arms and accoutrements, and, as appeared after, loaded; and that they had posted some men in a dwelling and Meeting-house.*

Our troops advanced towards them, without any intention of injuring them, further than to inquire the reason of their being thus assembled, and, if not satisfactory, to have secured their arms; but they in confusion went off, principally to the left, only one of them fired before he went off, and three or four more jumped over a wall and fired from behind it among the soldiers; on which the troops returned it, and killed several of them.

They likewise fired on the soldiers from the Meeting and dwelling-house. We had one man wounded, and Major Pitcairn's horse shot in two places. Rather earlier than this, on the road, a country man from behind a wall had snapped his piece at Lieutenants Adair and Sutherland, but it flashed and did not go off. After this we saw some in the woods, but marched on to Concord without anything further happening.

While at Concord we saw vast numbers assembling in many parts; at one of the bridges they marched down, with a very considerable body, on the light infantry posted there. On their coming pretty near, one of our men fired on them, which they returned; on which an action ensued, and some few were killed and wounded. In this affair, it appears that after the bridge was quitted, they scalped and otherwise ill-treated one or two of the men who were either killed or severely wounded, being seen by a party that marched by soon after.

At Concord we found very few inhabitants in the town; those we met with both Major Pitcairn and myself took all possible pains to convince that we meant them no injury, and that if they opened their doors when required to search for military stores, not the slightest mischief would be done. We had opportunities of convincing them of our good intentions, but they were sulky; and one of them even struck Major Pitcairn.

On our leaving Concord to return to Boston, they began to fire on us from behind the walls, ditches, trees, etc., which, as we marched, increased to a very great degree, and continued without the intermission of five minutes altogether, for, I believe, upwards of eighteen miles; so that I can't think but it must have been a preconcerted scheme in them, to attack the King's troops the first favorable opportunity that offered, otherwise, I think they could not, in so short a time as from our marching out, have raised such a numerous body, and for so great a space of ground. Notwithstanding the enemy's numbers, they did not make one gallant effort during so long an action, though our men were so very much fatigued, but kept under cover.

I have the honor, etc.

F. Smith, Lt-Col. 10th Foot.

Above: British munitions on display at Fort William Henry.

Opposite, top: British army sabers on display at Fort William Henry.

Opposite, bottom: British swords on display at Fort William Henry.

When word about what happened at Lexington and Concord reached Great Britain, the news was taken to be nothing more than colonial propaganda. But as other events began to unfold, it became clear that the Americans were serious about not reconciling with the mother country and their desire for sovereignty. The British government hadn't taken the threats of revolution seriously and thus did not initially have a plan in place to go to war with the colonists. Parliament, which had gone on its summer break, reconvened after the events at Lexington and Concord to discuss plans to increase the size of its army and planned for a long campaign.

After the events at Lexington and Concord, the citizens of Massachusetts wanted to dispel the British from Boston but were lacking in the weaponry to do so. Heavy artillery was unavailable at the time to colonial militias, but cannons were in ample supply at the weakly manned British forts of Fort Ticonderoga and Crown Point. With that knowledge in mind, the Americans devised a plan to seize the cannons and bring them to Boston.

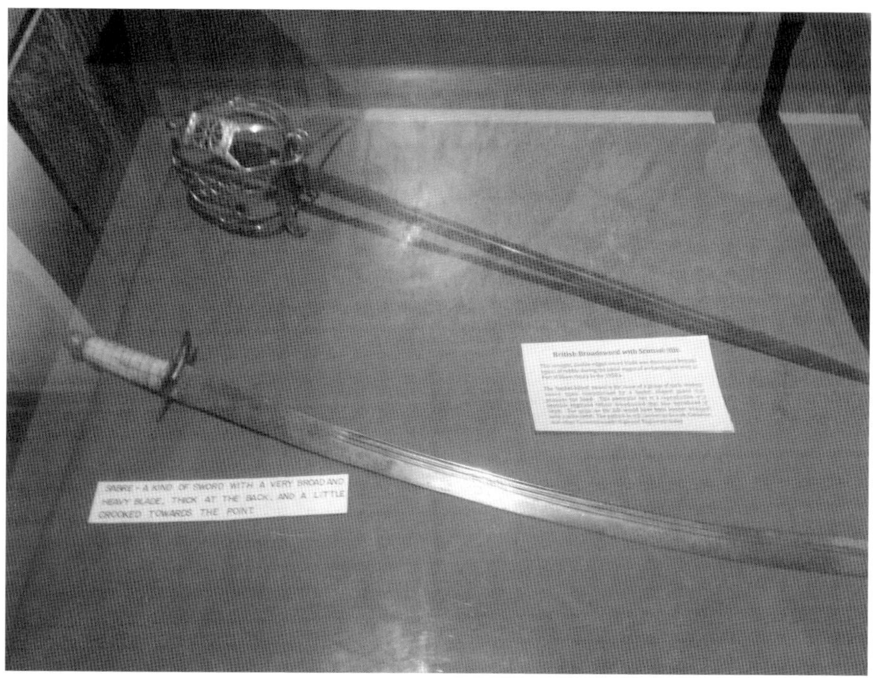
SABRE - A KIND OF SWORD WITH A VERY BROAD AND
HEAVY BLADE, THICK AT THE BACK, AND A LITTLE
CROOKED TOWARDS THE POINT

ARGENTINE MODEL 1891
FRENCH MODEL 1874

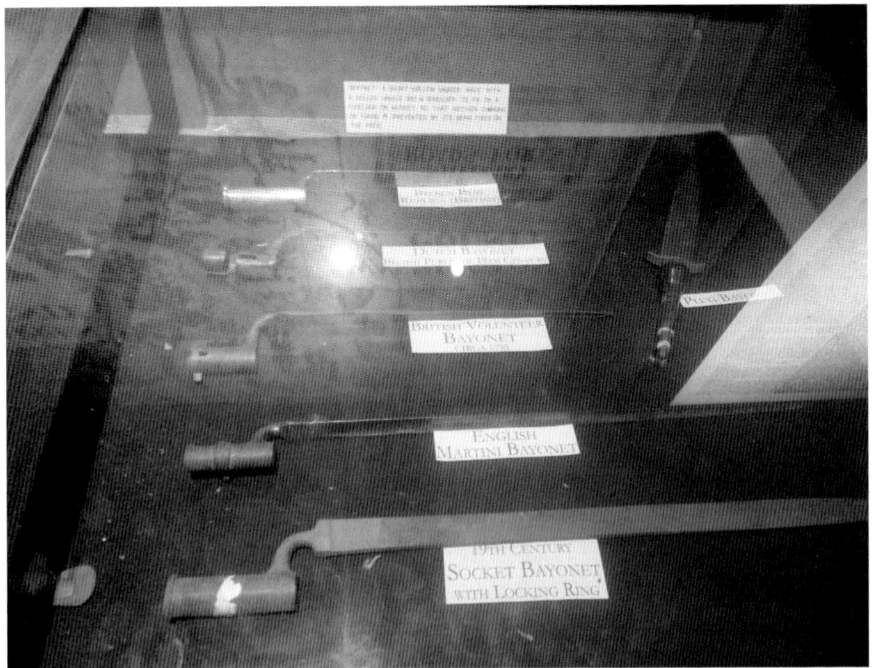

British bayonets on display at Fort William Henry.

As early as 1767, just after the Seven Years' War had come to an official end, Sir Guy Carleton, the governor of Quebec, had spoken of the importance of maintaining the fortifications that were in the British possession in North America, especially those that were along the vital waterways. Carleton's words went unheeded, and Forts Ticonderoga and Crown Point had fallen into disrepair. As the situation in Massachusetts grew increasingly dire, in 1774, British military leader Frederick Haldimand requested an inspection of the forts. A report was returned to him stating that the fort was in ruinous conditions. Haldimand, in turn, wrote to Parliament proposing that two regiments be moved from Canada to Fort Crown Point to aid in the rebuilding of the forts, which he stated would allow for continued communication among the New England colonies, Canada and Great Britain and provide access to the colonial borderland settlements. Haldimand's request went unmet by Parliament. Later in 1774, as tensions continued to flare in the New England colonies, another British officer said that the forts were in a state of disadvantage in their condition and requested that small repairs be made but to "as little an expense as possible." On November 2, 1774, word had finally arrived by the British government granting permission to go ahead with the necessary repairs to the forts. However, the winter months were fast approaching in the Upstate New York region, and those repairs were not made.

With the fort in disarray and loaded with more than one hundred cannons and grapeshot for the heavy artillery, the remote Upstate New York Fort Ticonderoga was a prime target for the American rebels, who were desperate for arms and armaments in Boston.

Early in May 1775, Connecticut authorized Ethan Allen and two hundred Green Mountain Boys to attack the weakly garrisoned and poorly maintained Fort Ticonderoga to capture its cannons. Benedict Arnold, who arrived with a colonel's commission and orders from the Massachusetts Committee of Public Safety, also attempted to assume command of the attacks on Forts Ticonderoga and Crown Point. Both men had big personalities that mixed as well as oil and water, and fighting broke out between the two officers about who should assume command for the mission's duration. After a heated dispute, the men decided to command the mission together. In the early morning hours of May 10, 1775, Ethan Allen, Benedict Arnold and eighty-one soldiers marched into Fort Ticonderoga and took the British garrison by surprise, famously without firing a shot. Along with Fort Ticonderoga, Allen and Arnold quickly captured the fort at Crown Point in May 1775.

The artillery seized from the captured forts was put in the hands of Henry Knox, who would move fifty-nine of the cannons to Boston to aid in dispelling the British from the city. Knox's "Noble Train" was technically complicated but overall successful. In just fifty-six days, Knox and the Americans with him moved the cannons from Fort Ticonderoga to the Heights of Dorchester, an approximately three-hundred-mile trek, which began in December 1775. The siege of Boston by the American rebels was successful in driving the British out of the area. The British retreated to Halifax, Nova Scotia, on March 17, 1776.

After the capture of the forts at Ticonderoga and Crown Point, the Americans under Benedict Arnold and Ethan Allen continued their successful takeover of the area. At the southern end of Lake Champlain was the Loyalist settlement of Skenesborough (present-day Whitehall), established in 1759 by Philip Skene. This was quickly taken by the Americans as well. Skenesborough was the first permanent settlement in the Lake Champlain region and was an important maritime trade settlement, as ships could move through Lake Champlain to get to Quebec and could trade with the British West Indies. At Skenesborough, the Americans captured Philip Skene's schooner, *Katharine*, and commissioned it for their

Top: Fort Ticonderoga's exterior.

Bottom: The cannons overlooking Lake Champlain at Fort Ticonderoga.

own use as the first designated warship of what would become America's navy under its new name, *Liberty*. Benedict Arnold assumed command of *Liberty* and embarked to St. Johns, Canada, where he captured a sloop, *Betsy*, and renamed it *Enterprise*.

With the capture of Fort Ticonderoga, Crown Point, Skenesborough and two British ships, the Americans controlled a major waterway that brought them into the heart of Quebec. The Americans would use this advantage to launch an invasion of British Upper Canada.

AMERICAN INVASION OF CANADA

The victories at Fort Ticonderoga, Crown Point and Skenesborough gave the Americans confidence that they could convince their neighbors to the north, the Canadians, to join them in the fight for independence from British rule. But they were sorely mistaken. After the Canadians refused to side with the Americans, the Americans launched a two-pronged attack on Canada.

One army moved through the forests of Maine to Quebec, and the other army moved on Quebec, utilizing Lake Champlain as a water route for the invasion. Brigadier General Richard Montgomery was chosen to lead the first army through Maine; Benedict Arnold was chosen to lead the second army utilizing the lake.

Lieutenant Governor and Administrator of Quebec Sir Guy Carleton realized that the Americans were planning to invade Canada and moved the bulk of his forces to Montreal and Fort St. John in an attempt to block the American advance north from Lake Champlain to Quebec.

The Americans, under Montgomery, besieged Fort St. Jean in September 1775. Carleton attempted to relieve the fort, but his efforts failed, and the fort fell to the Americans on November 3. Carleton abandoned Montreal and Fort St. Jean and withdrew his forces to Quebec, where Benedict Arnold was already awaiting Montgomery's forces, which would arrive in December.

Under the cover of snowfall in the early morning hours of December 31, 1775, the American forces moved to attack Quebec. The British were ready for the advance and opened fire on the Americans. General Montgomery was killed in the assault, and after his men failed to penetrate Quebec's defenses, they were forced to retreat.

Benedict Arnold's forces did not fare much better. The British fired on his troops, causing a number of casualties and wounding Arnold in the leg. Patriot Daniel Morgan assumed command, but the Patriots ultimately called off their attack. Reinforcements from New York, Pennsylvania, Massachusetts, New Hampshire and Connecticut marched along the frozen Lake Champlain and the St. Lawrence River, but they were too late to save Arnold's and Montgomery's efforts to take Quebec.

With their attempt to capture Quebec squashed, the weakened American forces camped outside the city throughout the winter, attempting to maintain the siege despite disease and famine plaguing the battered army.

A Hasty Retreat and Lake Champlain's Fleets

The Americans stubbornly maintained their siege on Quebec in the early months of 1776, but Sir Guy Carleton knew that he would be receiving assistance from the British once the ice on Lake Champlain and the St. Lawrence River melted.

Lake Champlain as seen from Fort Ticonderoga.

As expected, in May 1776, a force of ten thousand British regulars and Hessian mercenary troops arrived in Quebec. The Americans, greatly outnumbered, were forced to make a hasty and disorganized retreat from Canada.

The Americans had captured and armed four vessels in 1775—*Liberty*, *Enterprise*, *Royal Savage* and *Revenge*—giving them the upper hand in the Champlain Valley in the summer of 1776, as the British lacked a naval fleet in the area at the time and were unable to advance southward following the American army. Throughout the summer of 1776, both the Americans and the British worked to assemble naval squadrons to take full control of Lake Champlain. The side that could take naval control of the lake would control of the entire valley.

Skenesborough, present-day Whitehall, New York, was chosen for the construction of the American naval fleet. By early October 1776, the fleet had sixteen vessels and was under the command of General Benedict Arnold, who personally funded much of the fleet's construction.

At the time the Americans were building up their fleet, the British fleet was also being constructed. Unbeknownst to the Americans, the British fleet was far superior, with bigger ships, more guns and professional forces with naval experience. It was commanded by Sir Guy Carleton and his nephew Captain Christopher Carleton.

On October 11, 1776, the American and British naval fleets engaged in combat in the vicinity of Valcour Island.

BATTLE OF VALCOUR ISLAND

In October 1776, the British under the command of General John Burgoyne were planning to invade America through Canada via Lake Champlain, where they would then be able to take the Hudson River to Albany. Under General William Howe and his brother Admiral Richard Howe, the British would take New York City; then the southern British army under General Howe would make its way north up the Hudson River to Albany. Together, the combined forces of Burgoyne and Howe would capture New York. Realizing that Lake Champlain and Lake George would be the British army's gateway to the north, the Americans made a commitment to stop the British advance on the lakes. As the British army began its advance, General John Sullivan and Benedict Arnold wrote to George Washington urging that Lake Champlain be secured by an American naval fleet. At Skenesborough (later renamed Whitehall), Sullivan, Arnold and Major General Philip Schuyler constructed the first American naval force, using the iron forge and sawmills in the town. The Americans had numerous issues with constructing their fleet, including shortages in iron and other construction equipment, shortages in shipbuilders willing to come to the area to assist with construction and a shortage of skilled sailors and marines. The British and Loyalist forces, on the other hand, were not lacking in these things when it came to the construction of their own fleet in the Lake Champlain region. Slowly, the Americans received the help they needed, and on October 11, 1776, as part of the American naval force lying in wait in Valcour Bay, they were alerted to the oncoming—and far superior—British fleet. It had had twice as many cannons, more ships and more trained sailors. As the two sides engaged in a running naval battle in Valcour Bay, the British also fired on the Americans from Valcour Island itself as well as from the shore of Lake Champlain.

The Battle of Valcour Island went back and forth and included devastating losses for both sides. At the start of the battle, the American ship *Royal Savage* ran aground and had to be abandoned. The British later captured the ship and burned it. The British ship *Carleton* took a savage beating, and most of its crew were killed or wounded. And a British gunboat was destroyed when a shot it sustained touched off its powder magazine, blowing up the ship. Fighting continued with the two naval forces bombarding each other. As the sun set, the British forces took refuge south of the American line, confident that they would secure a victory by morning. The Americans had other plans, and rather than resting for the night, Benedict Arnold led his fleet south through the British under the cover of darkness. When the morning came, Carleton moved toward where the American line had been and was surprised to find that the fleet was no longer there. Due to unkind winds, Carleton was unable to gain ground on the Americans, and Arnold was unable to increase space between his forces and the British, so the second day of battle was a bust. October 13 saw the naval battle resume. The British caught up with the Americans at Split Rock, and Arnold made the strategic choice to run his fleet aground near Fort Crown Point, burn the fort and escape to Fort Ticonderoga.

The Americans and the British continued to engage each other, and the results were devastating for the Americans and brought destruction to nearby homes. A home belonging to a Patriot family headed by a man named Peter Ferris was reportedly hit by several cannonballs and grapeshot. As a consequence of assisting the Americans escape into the woods after their fleet was run aground, the British burned the Ferris home and farm and killed all of the cattle. The social implications of the Americans' failed attempt at the Battle of Valcour Island were the destruction of property by citizens who helped and supported the Patriot forces. Sir Guy Carleton and his nephew Sir Christopher Carleton, who were both involved in the Battle of Valcour Island, carried out raids in Upstate New York, destroying towns and villages where Patriots resided or where Patriot forces had the potential to obtain help from the local population.

Although the Americans lost the Battle of Valcour Island and the British under the Carletons carried out raids against American towns, it was too late in the year for the British to attempt to fight the Americans in Upstate New York again. If nothing else, the Battle of Valcour Island bought the Americans time to figure out a plan for a more successful fight against the British and Loyalist troops in New York's wilderness. The Americans had a naval force that was not a true rival to the British Royal Navy but was acceptable given the circumstances in which it was required.

Siege of Fort Ticonderoga

In the summer of 1777, as part of the events of what would be known as the Saratoga Campaign, the Americans and the British engaged each other one more time at Fort Ticonderoga.

The summer after their success at the Battle of Valcour Island, the British once again found themselves in the Lake Champlain region as they executed the early portion of a multipronged strategy under Major General John Burgoyne and Barrimore St. Leger. The plan was for the men to move south from Upper Canada to Albany, New York, where they planned to take control of the Hudson River and divide the colonies. In early July 1777, Burgoyne and his fighting force of 9,100 Regular, Loyalist, Hessian and Iroquois troops moved to retake Fort Ticonderoga from the Americans, who had fortified not only that site but also nearby Mount Hope. Mount Defiance, which overlooked the fort, was left undefended, and the British took note of this and used it to their benefit by secretly sending engineers up the mountain to clear an area for artillery that could be used in the siege.

At this time, Fort Ticonderoga was lightly manned and thus lightly defended. The Americans, who numbered four thousand under the command of Major General Arthur St. Clair, planned to defend the fort for as long as possible before they used a pontoon bridge to cross the lake to Mount Independence and withdraw to a safe distance from the British forces. Burgoyne's main force landed on the west side of Lake Champlain near the fort on June 30. His Hessian troops were ordered to march on the opposite shore of the lake toward Mount Independence, which threatened to cut off the American withdrawal route. Burgoyne noted that Sugar Loaf (now known as Mount Defiance), which overlooked the fort, was left undefended by the Americans. The British sent engineers up the mountain to clear an area that could be used in the siege of the fort. St. Clair noticed the British artillery on Sugar Loaf, ruining a possible surprise attack. Due to the lack of manpower, St. Clair decided to retreat from the fort and give up the strategic location rather than engage with the British. On July 5, under the cover of darkness, St. Clair moved his sick and wounded from the fort as his main force made its retreat, leading two hundred boats south through Mount Independence and Skenesborough. The British retook the fort without firing a shot, as their American counterparts had done in 1775. The British attacked the Americans at Hubbardton (in Vermont) and at Fort Anne, New York (now Fort Ann).

British encampment at Fort Ticonderoga.

As a response to the end of the siege at Fort Ticonderoga, General Philip Schuyler wrote letters to General Washington to tell him of the loss and how valiantly the men fought. But the

British Regulars training at Fort Ticonderoga.

letters also indicated that the men lost everything they possessed at the siege and inquired of Washington to send "Tents for 4000 Men, 500 Camp Kettles: a Quantity of fixed musquet Ammunition, Cartridge-paper 12 pieces heavy Cannon with travelling Carriages 16 Field pieces and a considerable Quantity of Ammunition for them; a competent Number of Artillery Men, in Addition to Major Steven's Corps, so as to be sufficient to manage the Artillery; All the Implements necessary to the Artillery; Horses, Harness and Drivers; about 600 Intrenching Tools sorted, excluding pick axes of which we have a considerable Number." It was true that the Americans lost everything in the siege, and it was also true that military gear was not easy to come by. The Continental Congress had failed to provide the Continental army with the necessities it needed at the time of the war, such as gear, money and even an adequate number of able-bodied men willing to fight and die for the idea of America. After receiving these letters, Washington was furious that Fort Ticonderoga had been abandoned by its defenders so easily, without a single shot being fired and without a sustained siege. St. Clair was stripped of his command and was court-martialed in 1778, along with his superior officer, General Philip Schuyler. Both men were exonerated from any wrongdoing but suffered tarnished reputations because of the actions taken at Fort Ticonderoga in 1777.

The Americans, compared to their British and Loyalist counterparts, were underpaid, undermanned and undersupplied for the duration of the war, only achieving some relief after the Battle of Saratoga with the help of the French, Spanish and Dutch.

The British held Fort Ticonderoga until October 1777, and under Burgoyne's orders, the fort was burned so it could not be utilized by the Americans as a military fortress during the remainder of the war. The British abandoned the fort for a time. In 1781, the British rebuilt the fort and used it to garrison both soldiers and civilians as they retreated from New York to Upper Canada, where many Loyalists would settle after the war's conclusion.

6

THE LAKE GEORGE REGION

Lake George, particularly the Village of Lake George, is a popular tourist area in Upstate New York. Nicknamed the "Queen of American Lakes," Lake George is a long, narrow lake located at the southeast base of the Adirondack Mountains. The massive lake lies within the upper region of the Great Appalachian Valley and drains northward to the Lake Champlain and St. Lawrence River basins. The lake extends just over thirty-two miles from north to south, with Fort William Henry at its southern bank and Fort Ticonderoga to the north. It is situated within the direct land route from Albany, New York, to Montreal, Quebec. This made the Lake George region vital during both the Seven Years' War and the American War for Independence.

Although the region played more of a role during the Seven Years' War, the Lake George region did see conflict during the Revolutionary War, in a little-known event in 1777 at Diamond Island.

Diamond Island's Forgotten Battle

During General John Burgoyne's 1777 campaign, known as the Saratoga Campaign, his army made its way through New York from Canada with the ultimate goal of reaching Albany, but his progress stalled near Skenesborough (present-day Whitehall, New York). The campaign was

The *Minihaha* steamboat on Lake George.

taking longer than Burgoyne had anticipated, and his supplies were running low. Unable to supply his large army by living off the land, Burgoyne had to create a supply line in the area, which ran from the ruins of the forgotten Fort George at the southern end of Lake George and Fort Ticonderoga. Between the two forts was Diamond Island, which was guarded by two companies of the Forty-Seventh Regiment of Foot under the command of Captain Thomas Aubrey and housed a British-Loyalist supply depot.

The Americans had been following Burgoyne's movements closely and had a plan to flank Burgoyne's sides. In mid-September, when Burgoyne was nearing the Schuylerville-Stillwater area, American major general Philip Schuyler suggested keeping some militia forces in Vermont to flank Burgoyne. Following suit, Major General Horatio Gates ordered Major General Benjamin Lincoln to flank Burgoyne's rear.

With two thousand men under his command, Lincoln divided his brigade into three commands of about five hundred men each. The first American brigade, under Colonel Benjamin Woodbridge, was sent to Skenesborough. The second, under Colonel Samuel Johnson, marched to Mount Independence, where it engaged with about three hundred German yagers who had been ordered to guard that position. And the third, under Colonel John Brown, made a gutsy attempt to take Fort Ticonderoga before marching toward Diamond Island.

The American flotilla consisted of one sloop with three mounted guns, two gunboats each with one cannon and seventeen bateaux, all carrying about 420 men to their goal of Diamond Island. Although Brown wanted to attack the British position on September 23, a storm forced the Americans to take cover during the night. But the flotilla set sail again the following morning from Sabbath Day Point.

Brown's command reached Diamond Island around 9:00 a.m. Unfortunately for the Americans, the Forty-Seventh Regiment of Foot was lying in wait. Captain Aubrey, who fought at the Battle of Bunker Hill, heard about the Americans making their advance toward Diamond Island and, with just over thirty hours before the Americans were set to make their landfall, had his forces construct breastworks and position surplus cannons that Burgoyne had left behind for them. The British were able to fire on the militiamen from both sides, with Brown's forces putting up a fight of their own. After two hours, however, Brown had to give up the fight when two of his own mounted cannons ceased to work after the continuous firing.

Brown's sloop had taken on water and had to be towed by one of the other boats to the east side of Lake George, near present-day Van Warner's Bay. Brown burned the boats and baggage before leading his men toward Skenesborough. According to Loyalist accounts, that's not where the story ends. The commander of Fort George, Lieutenant George Irwine, reported to Burgoyne that Aubrey's forces pursued Brown's forces and captured an abandoned gunboat and ammunition.

Lake Luzerne in the American Revolution

In Upstate New York, several towns in the Lake George region were born during the 1760s. In the 1770s, these towns would suffer at the hands of the very barons who had purchased the land.

Ebenezer Jessup was born in July 1739 and was the younger brother of Edward Jessup, who was born in 1736. The brothers spent their early childhood in Stamford and Fairfield, Connecticut, and moved to "Nine Partners" in Dutchess County in 1744. Both Jessups served in the Seven Years' War. Edward served as a captain in Colonel Jeffrey Amhearst's 1759

MAP OF

THE PATENT OF

KAYADEROSSERAS

SCALE: 1" = 300 ch.

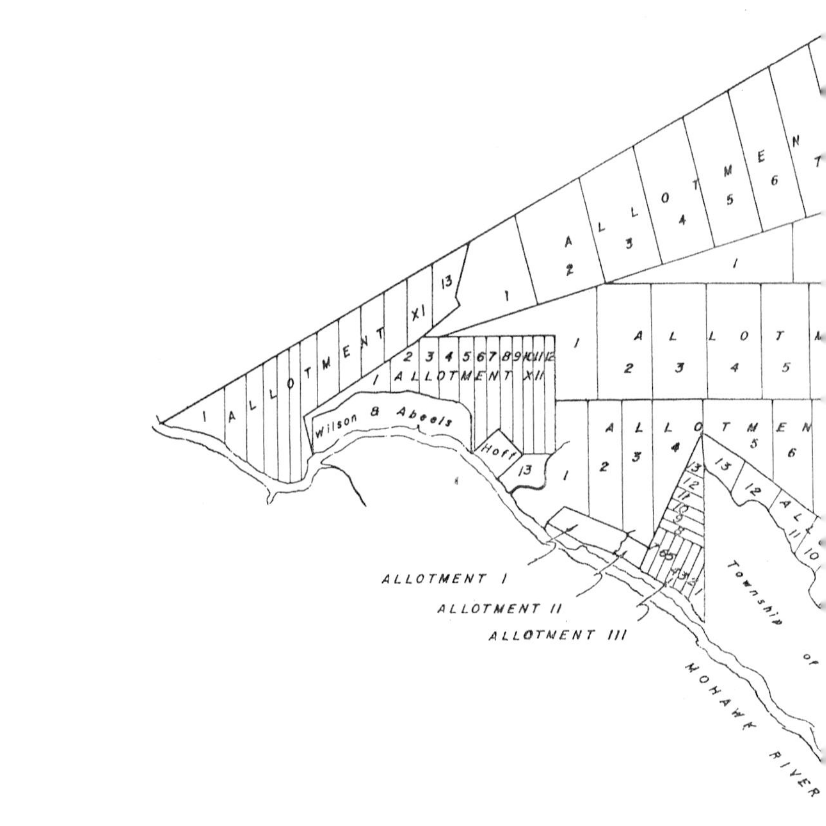

Map of the Kayaderosseras Patent. *Photo credit: Wiki Commons.*

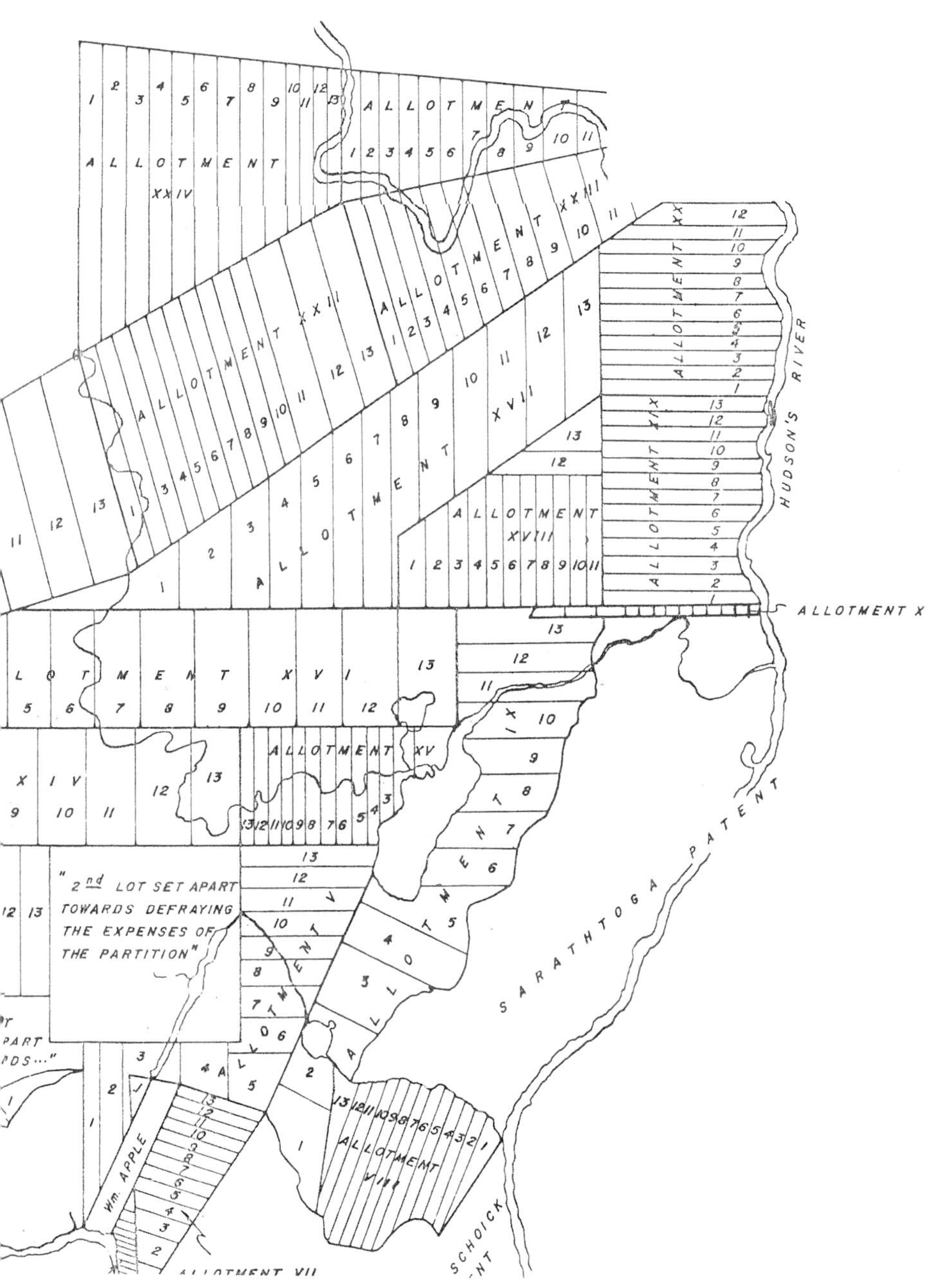
ALLOTMENT
ALLOTMENT XXIV
ALLOTMENT XXII
ALLOTMENT XXIII
ALLOTMENT XX
ALLOTMENT XIX
HUDSON'S RIVER
ALLOTMENT XVII
ALLOTMENT XVIII
ALLOTMENT
ALLOTMENT X
LOTMENT XVI
ALLOTMENT XV
XIV
IX
"2nd LOT SET APART TOWARDS DEFRAYING THE EXPENSES OF THE PARTITION"
ALLOTMENT V
ALLOTMENT VI
ALLOTMENT
ALLOTMENT VIII
SARATHTOGA PATENT
Wm. APPLE
SCHOICK

campaign in the Lake Champlain region, and it was then that he saw value in the land, as it was heavy in lumber, a vital natural resource. As the war drew to a close and the Lake George and Upper Hudson River regions were considered safe again for occupation, Edward and Ebenezer both received land grants from the royal government of New York after their military services. Also in the mid-1760s, the brothers moved from Dutchess County, New York, to Albany and engaged in land speculation in the Hudson River Valley and the Lake George area. The Jessups became friendly with Sir William Johnson, who had built Fort William Henry on the southern end of Lake George during the French and Indian War and became the superintendent of Indian Affairs after building a close relationship with the Mohawks of New York. The Jessups purchased much of their land from Johnson and the Mohawks. Prior to the outbreak of the American Revolution, the Jessup brothers bought the land that would become the towns of Lake Luzerne, Hadley, Corinth, Warrensburg, Thurman, Chestertown and Johnsburg. In 1772, the Jessups purchased more than eight hundred thousand acres from the Totten and Crossfield Purchase, which encompassed much of present-day Hamilton and Essex Counties. With the land, the Jessups built sawmills and rafted logs. They established a community named Jessup's Landing (today, the village of Corinth) and maintained a ferry and a road that followed the river upstream to Jessup's Falls (today, Rockwell Falls) between Lake Luzerne and Hadley. Their vast landholdings added up to over one million acres and encompassed nearly all of what is now northern and western Warren, Hamilton and Essex Counties. With the huge landholdings, the brothers became the first great lumber barons of the Adirondacks.

By 1770, Edward and Ebenezer had settled on one of their land grants on the Hudson River about ten miles northeast of Glens Falls. The brothers built luxurious log homes and were known for lavishly entertaining guests in "the wilderness." But tensions among colonists were running high, even in 1770.

The Jessups were successful in the Adirondack region when it came to purchasing land and establishing hamlets, towns and villages, but in the mid-1770s, when tensions were boiling over between Loyalists and Patriots, the people began to turn on the brothers. And the Jessups turned on the people living on their land. During the winter months of 1775, despite the war not yet having been officially declared, the colonists began to destroy property belonging to the Jessups, burning the mills and destroying the ferry. The mills that managed to survive were closed down, and the workers were laid off and provisions packed. As other Loyalists experienced at this time, the

Jessups faced threats of arrest and death. Edward and Ebenezer escaped to Canada by snowshoeing up the Sacandaga River, meeting up with John Johnson and other Loyalists also fleeing New York at Fish House in Northampton. From there, the fleeing party continued up the West Branch and over the Long Lake Military Road to Canada.

In the summer of 1776, Sir Guy Carleton was successful in driving American forces out of Quebec, and the Jessups led a party of eighty Loyalists to Crown Point. The Jessup party became attached to Sir John Johnson's King's Royal Regiment of New York.

In May 1777, Edward Jessup found himself in hot water. On May 6, Colonel Gordon, in command of the Continental militia in the Ball's Town district, pursued and captured thirty-one Loyalists on or near the Jessup Patent. All thirty-one Loyalists admitted that they were on their way to join General John Burgoyne's army and escape taking the oath of allegiance to Congress. Edward Jessup, however, was hotly pursued by Gordon and his militia. To evade capture, Jessup leaped across a gorge in the Hudson where the water was only twelve feet in width. He then made his way across Queensbury by an old road that ran parallel to the present route from French Mountain to Fort Ann(e). This trail would have taken Jessup over West Mountain and crossed the military trail leading from Fort George to Fort Edward. From Queensbury to Fort Ann(e), Jessup would have sought to camp on high ground above the wetlands in the vicinity of present-day Route 149. In the Fort Ann(e) area, a stream known as Halfway Brook (because it was halfway between Fort Edward and Fort George) joins Wood Creek leading to Skenesborough (Whitehall). Jessup would then have continued northward through Skenesborough to meet with Burgoyne's army at Willsborough Falls. Edward then joined Ebenezer, who had fled to join Burgoyne some months earlier and had received a commission in Burgoyne's army.

In the summer of 1777, General Gates dispatched militiamen under a Lieutenant Ellis to raid the Jessup Patent. Although the patent had already been thoroughly raided by the Americans, they thought it beneficial to conduct another raid. The Loyalist leaders in the Jessup Patent had fled in previous years, but the militiamen under Ellis destroyed the houses, burned the grain fields and pillaged the Jessup homestead.

As for the Jessup brothers themselves, Lieutenant Colonel Ebenezer and Captain Edward led the King's Loyal American corps to take part in General John Burgoyne's 1777 campaign. With the goal of capturing the Hudson River via Albany utilizing a multipronged strategy, this campaign, known now as the Saratoga Campaign, failed with the October surrender of Burgoyne's army to the Americans under General Gates. Edward and Ebenezer were among those who surrendered at Saratoga and marched north to Canada.

While in Canada for the winter, the British plan to raid the New York frontier and various key positions came to fruition.

On October 1, 1778, Major Christopher Carleton led a detachment of 800 British Regulars with the Twenty-Ninth Regiment, a company of German levies, 300 Loyalists and 175 Native American warriors on raids across New York. Colonel Ebenezer Jessup led the Loyalist battalion that acted as guides in New York and ensured that no farmhouse, no matter how isolated from civilization, remained unscathed.

In 1779, the Jessup brothers were included in a list of Loyalists who had attained the charge of treason by New York. The consequence of this charge was death should either, or both, of the Jessups be caught by Patriots within New York's borders. The brothers also had all of their property and landholdings seized by the State of New York. Ebenezer feared for his safety and moved with his family to Ontario. Edward, however, did not flee to Canada. In November 1781, he was named major commandant of a new corps of Loyal Rangers. This new unit was known colloquially as "Jessup's Rangers." They were present at the British raid on Ball's Town and perpetrated raids against the settlements in Queensbury, Glens Falls, Kingsbury, Fort Edward and Fort Ann(e).

Edward Jessup did not play a major role in the raid on Ball's Town. He and his Rangers participated in the raid under the command of Major Christopher Carleton. Jessup and his Rangers were familiar with the area they were raiding, as they had at one time lived in the area. In October 1780, the rangers moved with Carleton south along Lake Champlain, past the unmanned Fort Ticonderoga and arrived at Skenesborough (Whitehall) on October 8. The following day, they moved on the ramshackle and undermanned Fort Anne. The fort was under the command of Captain Adiel Sherwood, who, on hearing of Carleton and Jessup's advance, sent out a scouting party to see what he and his seventy-four men would be up against. This party did not have the chance to return to Sherwood, as it was ambushed by Iroquois warriors under Carleton's command, who captured and/or killed most of the men in the party. Jessup's Rangers were present to receive the surrender of Fort Anne and moved on to attack Fort George with Carleton. From there, Jessup and his men attacked Kingsbury, Queensbury and Glens Falls by razing the settlements to the ground. After this raid, Edward Jessup and his men made their way back to Canada, where they engaged in the construction of fortifications in and around Montreal and the lower Lake Champlain region.

In the fall of 1781, Edward Jessup led his own series of raids in Upstate New York. Once again, the Queensbury area was hit particularly hard. The Oneida Hamlet, as Queensbury was once called, was first settled about 1763 after the Seven Years' War had ravaged the area. These first settlers established their homesteads around the modern streets of Ridge Road, Glenwood Avenue and Hovey Pond. These first settlers and those who remained in the area at the time of the American Revolution were Quakers. Sometimes known as the Religious Society of Friends, the Quakers were pacifists. Despite Quaker antiwar leanings, the British believed their farms and homesteads to be threats to their cause to preserve the colonies. Believing that these homes could be used to benefit the Patriot troops in the area, Jessup and his rangers marched on Queensbury and burned the town to the ground a second time. Unfortunately, there is not much detailed information about the Jessup raid on Queensbury. British records remain spotty, as they did not consider the actions of American-born Loyalists to be on par with those born in Great Britain. The Americans did not keep accurate records on the smaller actions the Loyalist troops took against them. Despite the lack of details known about this raid, this second raid caused people to fear for their lives and leave the area. The destruction of farmland and cattle led to limited grain and meat, which was detrimental to the armies of both sides of the war as well as for the few families who opted to remain in the area.

In April 1783, with the official conclusion of the American Revolution, Edward Jessup's corps of Loyal Rangers was ordered to disband by the end of December of that year. As for Ebenezer, after the war he unsuccessfully petitioned for compensation for the property lost as a result of his support for the Crown. All of the land the Jessups owned prior to the outbreak of the Revolution was removed from their possession by the government of the State of New York. Like the Jessups, most New York Loyalists who did not take an oath of allegiance to the new American government were dispossessed of their landholdings. But the Jessups continued their legacy as land barons in their new lives as citizens of Upper Canada. At the conclusion of the war, Edward and some of his soldiers settled in Canada along the St. Lawrence River where Jessup would found the town of Prescott around 1810. Jessup and remnants of his rangers were also allotted townships; these became the towns of Edwardsburg, Augusta, Elizabethtown and Ernestown. In the fall of 1784, Edward Jessup followed in his brother's footsteps and traveled to London to submit his own petition for compensation to recuperate losses during the American Revolution. Like his brother's, his petition was unsuccessful.

Despite the actions of the brothers, their family name continues to have some prominence in New York. In the town of Lake Luzerne, there is a marker across the street from the Kinnear Museum stating that the town was part of a 4,100-acre patent granted to the Jessups. And in the town of Corinth, the local swimming area is known as Jessup's Landing, the original name for the settlement. The Jessups, particularly Edward, continued land speculation in Canada. As a military member of rank at the conclusion of the war, Edward was awarded land in the amount of 1,200 acres, and he continued to apply for land grants and was awarded another 3,800 acres in Ontario as well as a considerable amount of land in Sorel. He also held office as the executive council of Upper Canada, as a judge of the Court of Common Pleas and as lieutenant colonel of the militias of Edwardsburg, Augusta and Elizabethtown. Jessup was successful in life, and he saw his son succeed as well, helping his father establish the town of Prescott. Following Prescott's founding, much of the area, including Edward Jessup's own home, was taken over by the army, which built Fort Wellington, a War of 1812 fort, on the property. Edward passed away shortly after, in February 1816, having been bedridden for several years.

The American Revolution came to an end in 1783 with the surrender of British general Charles Cornwallis to American general George Washington in Yorktown, Virginia. With the end of the war came the end of the British raids in New York. Raiding forces disbanded at the end of the following year, and the former Loyalists struggled in the wake of this action. Many left the states and made lives for themselves in Upper Canada. Some moved across the pond and lived in Britain, while others continued to live in their home states. What the bulk of these former Loyalists experienced after the war was not a happy beginning in a new nation. Instead, they saw the dispossession of their property and suffered banishment from their home states.

During the American Revolution, many states passed a series of laws that allowed them to seize property belonging to known Loyalists. These confiscation laws, as they were called, criminalized dissent against the revolution, punishing those who chose the "wrong side." These laws also served as a means of banishing known Loyalists from New York State if they did not leave the state voluntarily, as many had done both during and after the Revolutionary War. For example, the Jessup brothers of Upstate New York fled to Canada before the war came to an end, and the more than one million acres of land they owned in present-day Warren County was forfeited to the state, becoming the towns of Lake Luzerne, Corinth, Warrensburg, Thurman, Chestertown and Johnstown. Per the confiscation laws, the properties were either sold for profit or redistributed to the community. At this time, New York built one of the strongest property-seizure mechanisms, and the act of depriving some people of their property became legitimized.

The act of seizing Loyalist properties and either auctioning off or redistributing the lands began as early as 1777, and the most aggressive of these confiscation laws was passed in October 1779. This law, referred to as the Forfeiture Act, included a list of New York Loyalists, both prominent and little known, and stated that these individuals had forfeited their property and their right to own property in the state, that they had been barred from living in the state and that the state had been given the power the sell the forfeited property for profit.

Similar laws in the very early 1800s got the public involved with the process of property seizure. If a New Yorker could prove to the surveyor general that there was property that belonged to once-treasonous individuals that had not yet been sold, the person who brought the property to the attention of the surveyor general would be granted 25 percent of its value when the land was sold.

As can be imagined, individuals fought against the forfeiture and confiscation acts, taking the matter to the courts. A young New York lawyer named Alexander Hamilton, later the first secretary of the treasury of the United States, is credited with helping former Loyalists reclaim their seized property. The reasoning behind Hamilton's assistance was that many of the former Loyalists were very wealthy, and he believed that if they were to reclaim their property and live in the new United States, their wealth would help bolster the economy. Hamilton believed that instead of banishing former Loyalists, they should be integrated into the new American society. To some extent, former Loyalists who chose to stay in New York were able to become a part of the new nation.

Lake Luzerne and Ivy Island, in the heart of the town, on a foggy morning.

In what we now know as Hadley and Lake Luzerne, Edward and Ebenezer were subjected to these confiscation laws. These towns saw their borders and names

Left: The waterfall at Mill Park in Lake Luzerne.

Right: The river at Mill Park in Lake Luzerne.

changed. On April 10, 1792, land was taken from neighboring Queensbury and renamed the town of Fairfield. It would not be until April 6, 1808, that the town was named Luzerne in honor of Anne-César de La Luzerne, a major general in the French Royal Army who also served as an official French diplomatic representative to the United States. He spent a considerable amount of time in Philadelphia. A county in Pennsylvania is named after him. It wouldn't be until 1963 that legislation was passed to rename the community the Town of Lake Luzerne.

ALTHOUGH MOST OF THE military activity in the Lake George area happened during the Seven Years' War, the few actions that did take place during the American Revolution, and the lives lost, cannot be ignored in history or in historiography. The Lake George region was a crossroads for the Revolution, as forces from both sides of the conflict made their way through the area and engaged each other briefly.

7

THE SARATOGA CAMPAIGN AND THE WAR'S TURNING POINT

One of the most important military campaigns of the American War for Independence was General John Burgoyne's 1777 campaign. The British and Loyalist forces realized the importance of New York as a vital Middle Colony. If they could take over strategic features, such as the Hudson River, New York would fall, and it would be only a matter of time before the other colonies were subdued as well.

Burgoyne's plan was different from what actually happened. The original plan was a three-pronged attack from Canada and British-occupied New York City to capture the Hudson River at Albany. Lieutenant General John Burgoyne commanded one prong; Major General Barrimore St. Leger commanded a second prong; and General William Howe was supposed to command a prong from New York City. But there were complications, and he didn't receive the message until it was too late.

The plan for what would become known as the Saratoga Campaign was made in 1776. Toward the end of that year, it was growing increasingly evident that pacifying New England was nearly impossible due to the large population of Patriots. Because of this, a plan to divide and isolate the various colonies was seen as beneficial for the British if it could be carried out successfully.

In December 1776, Lieutenant General John Burgoyne met with Lord George Germain, the British secretary of state for the colonies, to devise a strategy for 1777. There were two main British forces in North America at

The American lines at Saratoga National Battlefield Park.

the time the plan was being made: Major General Sir Guy Carleton's forces in Quebec and General William Howe's forces in New York City.

General Howe strategized a plan for capturing both Albany, New York, and the U.S. capital of Philadelphia. In his ambitious campaign, which he wrote about to Lord Germain, Howe stated that if he could be given ten thousand more men, he would capture Albany and then in the autumn of 1777 move to take Philadelphia. Shortly after sending the letter, Howe changed his mind. He realized that the reinforcements were not going to arrive in time to attack both Albany and Philadelphia and decided that he would make Philadelphia the primary target for his 1777 campaign, as he viewed it as a vulnerable location.

Howe sent his revised plan to Germaine. Historians are unclear about what happened next. Either Burgoyne wasn't notified of Howe's change of plans at all, or he was notified but not until his own campaign was underway. In any case, the third prong of Burgoyne's campaign was out of commission.

BURGOYNE'S PLAN TO CAPTURE ALBANY

Burgoyne proposed to isolate New England by an invasion from Quebec into New York. A similar plan had been attempted by Major General Sir Guy Carleton in 1776 after the Americans tried to invade Quebec, but due to the lateness of the season, Carleton stopped short of a full-scale invasion. In the southern colonies, Henry Clinton failed to capture Charlestown, South

Carolina. With these two British failures, Lord Germaine had great disdain for Carlton and Clinton, which placed Burgoyne in a favorable position to gain command of the northern 1777 campaign.

Burgoyne presented his written plan to Germaine in late February 1777, and it was approved, with Burgoyne gaining command of the primary expedition forces from Quebec.

Burgoyne's plan for invasion from Quebec had two components: he would lead the main force of about eight thousand men south from Montreal along Lake Champlain and down through the Hudson River Valley, while a second force of about two thousand men led by Barrimore St. Leger would move from Lake Ontario in the east and make its way to Albany by winding through the Mohawk River Valley. The two forces would converge on Albany, where they would link up with Howe's army and take control of the Hudson River. The successful control of the Lake Champlain–Lake George–Hudson River water routes would cut off the New England colonies from those in the South.

The issue with the plan, however, was with Howe's forces. Some historians argue that although Burgoyne was in London with Lord Germaine when his campaign plans were submitted and approved and that Howe's plans were submitted and approved first, Burgoyne may not have been notified of the change to Howe's Philadelphia plan. Regardless of who failed to notify Burgoyne of Howe's lack of support to move on Albany, Germaine did approve Howe's plans without including express directions for Howe to go to Albany. Interestingly, Germaine sent a copy of his instructions to Carleton, which did state that Burgoyne and St. Leger's army was supposed to link up with Howe's forces in Albany.

Germaine had written a letter to Howe, dated May 1777, stating that Howe's expedition should be carried out in a way that would allow him to attack Philadelphia as well as link up with the northern army. But Howe didn't receive the letter until after he left New York for the Chesapeake.

Howe could have made his expedition overland from New York through New Jersey and west to Philadelphia, or he could have sailed across the Delaware Bay, but he chose the more time-consuming route via the Chesapeake Bay.

Burgoyne returned to Quebec on May 6, 1777, with a letter in hand from Lord Germaine about the plan. In the plan, Carleton's role was extremely limited, with his operations being located strictly in Quebec. Not only that, but he felt as though he, not Burgoyne, should have been placed in command of the northern army. Carleton viewed these actions as a slight against him, and he resigned his position later in 1777.

The Campaign Begins

Most of Burgoyne's army had already arrived in Quebec in the spring of 1776 and helped push the Continental army out of Quebec.

The British northern army in Quebec, consisting of British regulars, also included several regiments of German Hessians and Brunswickers under the command of Baron Friedrich Adolf von Riedesel. Of these regular forces, about 200 British regulars and 300 to 400 Germans were assigned to St. Leger's prong of the expedition, and about 3,500 troops remained in Quebec to protect the province. The remaining men were assigned to Burgoyne.

The British ran into some difficulties with recruitment. The forces as previously described were supposed to be supplemented with as many as 2,000 militia enlisted in Quebec, but Carleton could raise only three small companies of 100 to 250 men each. Burgoyne was also hoping that at least 1,000 Native Americans would aid his expedition, but only about 500 joined him by the time he reached Crown Point.

The British also ran into difficulties when it came to transportation. The plan was to use water routes to move the troops and gear, so there were very few wagons and draft animals for the armies to use. In June 1777, Carleton issued orders to obtain carts. These were procured, but they were constructed poorly, and the teams selected to drive them were civilians, who were at high risk of desertion.

On June 14, 1777, Burgoyne's forces left from the vicinity of St. John's on the Richelieu River. Also in mid-June, St. Leger's forces left from the vicinity of Montreal.

In the summer of 1777, Burgoyne's and St. Leger's armies wove their way through New York with the goal of dividing the colonies. They left destruction in their wake, as Upstate New York and parts of Vermont were razed. The forces unknowingly made their way not to Albany as planned but instead toward the present-day villages of Schuylerville and Stillwater in Saratoga County.

The American Strategy

Burgoyne had grown increasingly worried that the Americans had caught wind of his plan, but it soon became obvious that that wasn't the case. The Americans, specifically the commander in chief, General George

Washington, along with General Horatio Gates and General Philip Schuyler, believed that if a British attack was going to happen in New York in 1777, it would come via the sea, as had happened at the Battle of Brooklyn Heights in 1776. Because of this, strategic locations in the vicinity of Lake Champlain and the Hudson River weren't fortified to the extent they should have been. For example, the garrisons of Fort Ticonderoga and elsewhere in the Hudson and Mohawk Valleys weren't increased. But in April 1777, General Schuyler made the decision to send a regiment under the command of Colonel Peter Gansevoort to Fort Stanwix as a means of deterring British movements in the Mohawk Valley. Washington ordered four regiments to be sent to Peekskill, New York, located about fifty miles north of New York City in Westchester County. These regiments could be moved to the north or south based on British movements.

In the late spring and early summer of 1777, the Americans were allocating troops to various areas in New York. Gansevoort commanded about 1,500 troops in the upper Mohawk Valley, General Israel Putnam commanded about 3,000 in the Hudson River highlands and Schuyler led about 4,000 troops in the vicinity of Lake Champlain.

Still, they weren't quite sure where the British would strike.

Fort Ticonderoga

Burgoyne's first hurdle in his 1777 campaign was the American defenses at the southern end of Lake Champlain, around Fort Ticonderoga.

Fort Ticonderoga was already a famous fort at the time. Built during the Seven Years' War by the French in 1755, it changed hands to the British in 1759, when the French abandoned the fort after the British failed to take it in 1758 in one of the bloodiest battles prior to the outbreak of the American Civil War. In May 1775, Fort Ticonderoga was taken by the combined forces of Ethan Allen and his Green Mountain Boys and Benedict Arnold and his troops from Massachusetts. In the winter of 1775, American Henry Knox transported artillery from Fort Ticonderoga and placed the cannons on high ground around Boston, forcing the British to evacuate the city in March 1776.

Fort Ticonderoga was the first line of defense for the Americans from a British invasion from Canada. Along with the fort, the French lines and the entrenchments surrounding the fort gave further protection. And the

Americans had constructed fortifications on Mount Independence, on the Vermont side of Lake Champlain. In order to advance toward his goal of Albany, Burgoyne would have to overcome these American positions.

By June 30, 1777, Burgoyne's army had settled at the undefended Fort Crown Point and devised a plan to split the eight-thousand-man army in two and attack from two points. One army, mostly of Brunswickers and Hessians under Baron Friedrich Adolf von Riedesel, landed on the east side of the lake with the goal of surrounding Mount Independence and cutting off the military highway that ran from Fort Ticonderoga across Lake Champlain and into New Hampshire. On the west side of the lake, Burgoyne's army would advance to surround and besiege Fort Ticonderoga.

General Arthur St. Clair, the American commander who was in charge of about three thousand troops at nearby Fort Ticonderoga, lacked intelligence on the strength of Burgoyne's army. St. Clair had been told by Schuyler to hold out as long as he could and planned two routes to retreat if he had to.

Although von Riedesel's advance was slowed by rough terrain, the British made fast work of their advance. On July 2, soldiers with Brigadier General Simon Fraser's Advance Corps captured the American position at Mount Hope. Over the course of the next three days, the British had Fort

Reenactors from the Thirty-Fifth Regiment of Foot, which was stationed at Fort William Henry in Lake George during the Seven Years' War.

Ticonderoga surrounded on its landed side and occupied Sugar Loaf Hill (now Mount Defiance) on July 5.

When St. Clair saw the British campfires on Sugar Loaf Hill, he ordered the immediate evacuation of Fort Ticonderoga and Mount Independence. Under the cover of darkness, he loaded supplies, wounded soldiers and noncombatants on a fleet of boats and sailed from Lake Champlain to Skenesborough. The fort's garrison retreated to Castleton, in present-day Vermont.

On July 6, seeing the fort abandoned, Burgoyne left a small garrison at Fort Ticonderoga and made the decision to follow the retreating Americans.

The Battle of Fort Anne

After the British siege of Fort Ticonderoga, the British and Americans engaged each other at Fort Ann(e), in present-day Fort Ann, New York. Long seen as a minor skirmish, the Battle of Fort Anne is now understood to be the Americans' first stand against Burgoyne's army, and its social implications included a change in American morale and a depletion of Burgoyne's forces as they continued to make their way south to Albany. These circumstances led to an increased feeling of patriotism and a growth in participation of New Yorkers in the Revolution, which benefited the American forces for the duration of the war.

The Battle of Fort Anne occurred on July 8, 1777, as the Americans were making their retreat from Fort Ticonderoga to Skenesborough, from which they would continue on to Fort Edward. Burgoyne's forces met up with the retreating Americans at numerous points (General Fraser and Riedesel engaged American forces at the Battle of Hubbardton on July 7 in present-day Vermont, and other British and Loyalist troops engaged Americans near Skenesborough). In a retreat from Skenesborough, the Americans set fire to the area, which served to slow the British advance, and the Americans made their way to Fort Anne. James Gray, a captain in a New Hampshire regiment, recorded the events of the battle on the back of a roster for his regiment.

> *Monday, 7th,—Got into Fort Anne at 6 in ye morning; everything in the utmost confusion; nothing to eat. General Philip Schuyler had sent 400 New York militia under Henry Van Rensselaer to Fort Anne to meet those*

retreating from Ticonderoga. At 11 o'clock A.M. [the same morning I arrived] *was ordered to take the Command of a party upon a scout and marched with 150 men besides 17 Rangers; had not marched from Garrison into the woods more than half a mile, after detaching my front, Rear and flanking Guards, when we met with a party of Regulars and gave them fire, which was Returned by the enemy, who then gave back. I then pursued them with close fire till they betook themselves to the top of a mountain. At the foot of this mountain we posted our selves and continued our fire until 6 P.M., when a reinforcement of 150 more joined me; but night approaching obliged me to return with my party to Garrison, after finding one of my party killed and 3 wounded, and three of the enemy killed by our first fire. Tuesday Morning, 8th,—Myself, with Capt. Hutchins, with the same number of men, marched to the aforesaid mountain and attacked the enemy very warmly. The engagement lasted about 2 hours, at which time the Commander of yo Garrison sent Colo. Ransleur* [Colonel Van Rensselaer] *with a small party of militia to reinforce us. We then advanced up the hill, where we found the enemy's surgeon dressing a Capts Leg. Those, with two of their wounded soldiers, we took and sent in, and a number of our own people, men & women, who were the day before cut off by the enemy, we retook. At last, finding out* [sic] *ammunition gone and none to be had in Garrison, ordered off my wounded and some of the dead, and formed a retreat. Much fatigued when I returned and found no refreshments, neither meat or drink; immediately a Council was called and the prisoners who were retaken brot upon examinationn, who gave information that an express just arrived before we made this second attack and gave the enemy intelligence that a reinforcement of 2000, with Indians, were near at hand to join them, at which time they were to make a general attack upon us. It was then determined upon to retreat to fort Edward, after setting fire the Garrison. Accordingly, the wounded were sent off, except one, who was one of my own Company; him the Surgeon thot proper not to order off, that he would soon expire, or that if he was likely to live, the enemy, when they took possession, would take care of him. This I knew not of till we were ordered to march, at which time I turned back alone (my Company being gone) to the rear of the Army, where I found him. I then picked up a tent & fastened it between two poles, laid him upon it, and hired four soldiers to carry him. I took their four guns with my own and carried them to fort Edward; this was about 3 o'clock P.M.; rained very hard; distance from Fort Anne to Fort Edward, 14 miles; arrived at Fort Edward at 10 in the Evening; no Barracks nor Tents to go into; therefore laid down in*

> *the rain and slept upon the ground; the fatigue of this day I believe I shall always remember. Colo Ransleur, wounded; Capt Weare, wounded; Ensign Walcutt, killed; Isaac Davis, a sergeant in my company, killed. Our loss in the two skirmishes about 15; the Enemy's unknown.*

The firsthand account of the events at the Battle of Fort Anne highlights what the soldiers endured over the course of the battle and the condition they were in as the surviving soldiers would make their way to garrison at Fort Edward.

Considering the engagements at Fort Anne, Skenesborough and Hubbardton as British victories, Burgoyne settled into the house of Loyalist Philip Skene at Skenesborough, where he decided his next steps while his army regrouped.

By July 10, Burgoyne had a plan for his next movements. The majority of his army was to march from Skenesborough to Fort Edward by going through Fort Anne, while the heavy artillery was to be transported down Lake George to Fort George (in the vicinity of the remains of Fort William Henry) and then follow the military road to Fort Edward.

The Americans heard about Burgoyne's movements, and Schuyler intended to make his movements to Fort Edward as difficult as possible. Using the garrison at Fort Edward, which numbered about 2,100 men, to fell large trees, destroy bridges and dam streams, the Americans slowed the British advance. The Americans made the British advance extremely difficult by also utilizing scorched-earth tactics, destroying farms and animals so the British troops couldn't use those as provisions.

THE MURDER OF JANE MCCREA AND AMERICAN PROPAGANDA IN THE REVOLUTIONARY WAR

While Burgoyne's troops were in the vicinity of Fort Edward, an incident shook both the British and the Americans and had a profound impact on the war.

Fort Edward was a town that had sprung up around where an abandoned British fort was located. The fort would come to garrison American troops and was a crossroads for American, British and Native American troops. The fort saw a lot of military movement between it and Rogers Island, where soldiers of both sides were trained for combat service between 1756 and 1781. Prior to the events of July 1777, however, no military activity in the vicinity of the fort had resulted in bloodshed since 1757, but that would change.

On July 27, 1777, a young woman named Jane McCrea was scalped by a band of Burgoyne's Iroquois mercenaries. According to legend, Jane was on the way to her wedding, traveling from the garrison town of Fort Edward to Fort Ticonderoga. To make matters worse, Jane McCrea was a Tory on her way to marry a British soldier. The indiscriminate killing of a Tory woman by Iroquois mercenaries employed by the British angered and embittered even the staunchest of Loyalist supporters. Jane McCrea's life prior to her death was a normal one for that era. Born in New Jersey around 1757, she was the daughter of a Scottish clergyman. She enjoyed reading, was kind and affectionate, was religious and was described by friends as uncommonly beautiful.

The murder of the young Loyalist bride caused controversies between both sides of the Revolutionary conflict and on both sides of the Atlantic. The American leader General Gates wrote Burgoyne a scathing letter, blaming him for the tragedy that befell Jane McCrea. Even Sir Edmund Burke, a Whig member of British Parliament, used the tragedy to rail against the policies of the Crown, particularly when it came to allowing its generals and Native mercenaries to run amok.

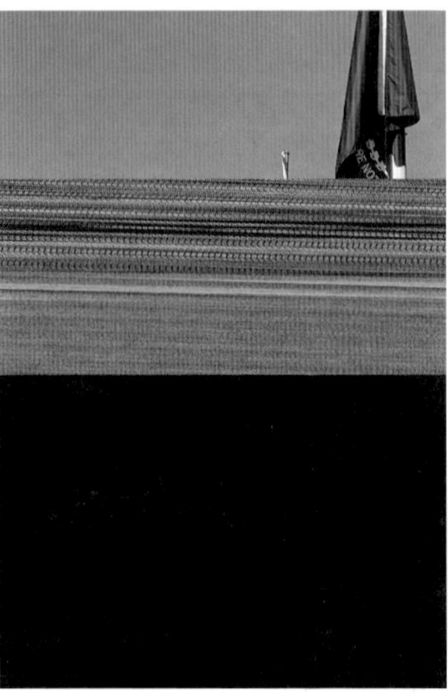

Top: A historical marker for the Jane McCrea House in Fort Edward, New York.

Bottom: Flags, including the British flag, along the bridge leading into Fort Edward, New York, from Moreau / South Glens Falls.

The murder of this young woman inspired New Yorkers to take up the Patriot cause, growing the ranks of the Continental army at a time when desertion was otherwise high. McCrea's murder resulted in major social effects in

Upstate New York. Much of the local population, who were Loyalist or otherwise apathetic to the Revolution as a whole, joined the cause and became fervent supporters of American patriotism in the wake of various Native American raids and indiscriminate murders. To them, the Loyalist cause was not one to support.

These circumstances had a major impact on Burgoyne, who was already struggling with enlisting local Loyalists to the British ranks. The increase of American Patriots in New York would turn out to play a role in a major strategic American victory.

The Siege of Fort Stanwix and the Battle of Oriskany

As Burgoyne's army continued its way south, the British forces under St. Leger were moving across the state as well. In August, the British under St. Leger besieged an American garrison, Fort Stanwix, near present-day Rome, New York.

The forces of Brevet Brigadier General Barry St. Leger came upon Fort Schuyler, more famously known as Fort Stanwix, in early August 1777. Fort Stanwix was situated in the upper Mohawk River Valley and guarded a critical area of the Mohawk River. But the British under St. Leger would be unable to take the fort in a head-on attack, so they chose to besiege the fort in order to force a surrender. The British had attempted to cut off a supply line from arriving to the fort but were unsuccessful. St. Leger demanded the surrender of the fort, but the American forces within, under Colonel Peter Gansevoort and Lieutenant Colonel Marinus Willet, refused. St. Leger's army surrounded the fort and fired on it with muskets and rifles, as they had been unable to access their heavily artillery, which was floated down the Wood Creek, stuck on the boats due to the Americans felling trees and burning bridges in the area. The British would besiege the fort for about twenty days before aid came to them. During that period, soldiers recorded what they experienced in their journals. One soldier, Ensign William Colbreth of the Third New York Regiment, wrote in his journal: "Augt. 12th. The Enemy kept out of sight all day and no firing from them till Noon when they gave us some Shott and Shells, without doing any damage. We Imagined the Enemy drew their Forces in the Day Time between us and Orisko, as we have not seen them so plenty these two or three Days as we are used to do. Neither do they trouble us all night, which gave our Troops an Opportunity of Resting. Augt. 13th. The Enemy were very peaceable all days towards Night when they Cannonaded and Bombarded for two Hours, during which Time a Shell broke a Soldier's Leg belonging to Colonel Millen's Detachment." As the days of the siege drew on, Ensign Colbreth continued to record the actions and inactions of the soldiers on both sides. In several of his journal entries, he described wounds the soldiers endured and any deaths that occurred due to soldiers being wounded in the siege. He also described several occurrences in which American soldiers deserted their posts.

Beginning on August 6, 1777, the Battle of Oriskany took place in the vicinity of Fort Stanwix. It would be one of the bloodiest battles of the American Revolution and was a result of Brigadier General Nicholas Herkimer and his men coming to the relief of the besieged Fort Stanwix. The Tryon County Militia and their Oneida allies were ambushed by Mohawk allies of the British under the command of Chief Joseph Brant as they were making their way to Fort Stanwix. In the ambush, Herkimer was injured in the leg but continued to lead his men as he sat under a tree, directing them to work in teams of two—while one soldier reloaded his musket or rifle, he was being covered by the other. Despite Herkimer's best efforts, the Americans were forced off the field. But the Tryon County Militia under Herkimer was able to assist the men stationed at Fort Stanwix. What seemed like an initial victory for St. Leger at the defeat of Herkimer's men proved to be a temporary loss, as his men wavered, unable to take the fort or force a surrender and giving up the fight on hearing word of Benedict Arnold and his men moving to assist Herkimer and the besieged fort.

Under Lieutenant Colonel Marinus Willet, raids were carried out on St. Leger's camps as they retreated. In one of the raids, a mailbag that was supposed to have been delivered to Fort Stanwix but was confiscated by St. Leger's men was returned to the fort. It contained a letter to Colonel Peter Gansevoort written by the woman he loved. When his men asked if he had plans to marry his love, Gansevoort responded that if they could get through battle alive, he would marry his love. On January 12, 1778, Colonel Gansevoort married Catherine "Katie" Van Schaik. As for Herkimer, he died on August 16, 1777, from wounds sustained in battle. But his legacy lived on in a song written shortly after the Battle of Oriskany, "General Herkimer's Battle," written by an author under the pen name "Juvinus."

Due to the great loss of life of the local militiamen, as well as the felling of trees, the burning of bridges and both sides burning down structures where the enemy could find cover, the area was devastated. Local families were prompted to leave due to the war and because of raids carried out by Chief Joseph Brant that lasted through the end of the war. The area was colloquially known as the "bread basket" of the state, as this was where the most farms, specifically for grains such as wheat, rye, oats and barley, were located. The grains produced on these farms were for the benefit of the families who ran them but also for the armies and citizens of the state. The lack of grain farming in the area as the war went on meant that the armies were not getting necessary rations at a time when the food supply, especially for the American forces, was already very low.

The Battle of Bennington

The Battle of Oriskany led to continued fighting in the area, and the Saratoga Campaign grew. Soon, another battle was underway in Walloomsac, New York, about ten miles from Bennington, Vermont.

The Battle of Bennington was the last skirmish before the Americans and the British faced off at the pivotal Battle of Saratoga. Taking place between August 14 and August 16, 1777, the Battle of Bennington resulted in a minor American victory, with Major General John Stark's forces defeating two detachments of General John Burgoyne's advancing army.

As a result of previous military engagements, the British found themselves low on supplies. They heard that there were stores in Bennington. The Americans, under Stark, attacked the British from

Top: Reenactors at Bennington, Vermont.

Bottom: The Bennington Monument.

multiple angles as they encamped near the Walloomsac River. Another detachment of Burgoyne's troops was sent to fight to help their outnumbered comrades. As the Americans were beaten back by the British, Colonel Seth Warner and his Green Mountain Boys came to Stark's aid. The Americans were able to overpower the British, who retreated in an unorganized manner.

A monument in Bennington, Vermont.

Many of Burgoyne's men who fought at the Battle of Bennington came from his Iroquois forces, and Bennington marked the beginning of the end for many of Burgoyne's men. With the devastating loss at Bennington, British, German and Iroquois desertion rates rose. This loss of able-bodied soldiers had a devastating effect on the British army and played a role in its defeat at Saratoga. After the Battle of Bennington, Patriot forces engaged in the torture and murder of captured British soldiers. In the aftermath of Bennington, the treatment of British captives at the hands of Americans indicated that the rules of engagement that had existed for battles and war were no longer regarded.

The Battles of Saratoga

The American victory at Bennington further halted the British advance. This allowed the Americans who had already reached Saratoga time to dig into the earth, creating breastworks and other earthworks to protect themselves. In September 1777, the first of the engagements at Saratoga, the Battle of Freeman's Farm, took place. The second engagement, the Battle of Bemis Heights, occurred in October 1777. Burgoyne's plan for the Saratoga Campaign was, once again, to head to Albany, then link up with British troops garrisoned in New York City. The British would then cut the American colonies in two. The area where the Battle of Saratoga would take place was chosen by General Horatio Gates to stop the British advance toward Albany. The land was owned by the Bemis and Freeman families, both Loyalists, as well as the Neilson family, who served in the American army.

On September 19, 1777, the British under Burgoyne and the Americans under Gates engaged each other in battle. The Americans had established themselves at Bemis Heights, which would become an important defensive position along the Hudson River. They had fortifications on the floodplain and cannons on the heights. Burgoyne's forces had been utilizing the Hudson River to transport supplies, and the American defenses on the heights were unavoidable. Learning of the defenses at Bemis Heights, Burgoyne moved his army inland to avoid the danger but collided with part of General Gates's army near the abandoned Freeman farm. During the fighting on September 19, the British were unable to gain ground or maintain momentum. Later in the day, German auxiliary troops under Baron von Riedesel turned the tide of the battle for the British. The baron's wife, Baroness von Riedesel, kept a journal throughout the war and wrote about the Battle of Freeman's Farm. She wrote that she feared for her husband's life when she realized he was a part of the battle. Two thousand British women and servants attended the battles at Saratoga, and the baroness's diary is an astonishing source, offering historians a look into the past and at what the women had to endure in the camp, as well as the personal thoughts of the baroness on the strategic Battle of Saratoga.

The British suffered heavy casualties at this first battle, and with supplies running dangerously low, Burgoyne made the conscious decision to wait for reinforcements and supplies from General Henry Clinton in New York City. As September turned to October, Burgoyne realized that Clinton's reinforcements would not be making their way to the Stillwater-Saratoga area. On October 7, Burgoyne tried to make another attack at the Battle of Bemis Heights. Benedict Arnold, who had been ordered to stay in his tent by General Gates after an argument, disobeyed the commanding officer and rallied his troops at Balcarres Redoubt and sustained an injury to his leg. The British were driven back and, under the cover of darkness, stacked their arms and retreated into Saratoga. On October 17, 1777, General John Burgoyne surrendered to General Horatio Gates, putting an end to the battles at Saratoga and the British strategy to take the Hudson River and divide the colonies—for a time.

In a letter to John Hancock, the president of the Continental Congress, dated October 12, 1777, General Horatio Gates described the events of the Battle of Freeman's Farm, the condition of his men and the whereabouts of General Burgoyne and his troops. Although the four-page letter has succumbed to age and wear and tear, with some words unable to be read now, a transcript of the letter reads as follows. [Please note that in the letter, the phrase *[object Object]* denotes that several words were illegible by the library/museum's transcribers:]

Campt at Saratoga Oct 12th 1777

Sir,

I have the satisfaction to acquaint your Excellency with the great success of the of the Army of the United States in the [[object Object]]

On the 7th just the heavy attacked [[object Object]] *Picked up on loss which decent* [[object Object]] *about the same hour of the day, and near* [[object Object]] *same spot of ground where that of the 19th of Sept was fought. From 3 o'clock in the Afternoon until almost Night the Conflict was very warm & bloody, when the heavy by a precipitate retreat determined the Fate of the Day leaving in our Hand eight pieces of Brass cannon, the Tents and Baggage of men Flying Army, a large quantity of* [[object Object]] *ammunition, a considerable number* [[object Object]] *wounded and Prisoner amongst* [[object Object]] *following principal officer* [[object Object]] *who commanded the artillery, Major Ackland who commanded the Corps of Grenadier, Capt. Money(?) who commanded L.M. Gnl and Sir Francis Clark principal Aide de Camp to his Excellency Genl Burgoyne. The loss upon our side is not more than killed and* [[object Object]] *wounded. Amongst the latter is the gallant Major Genl Arnold whose Leg was fractured by a Musket Ball as he was forcing the heavy's Breach Work(?). Too much Praise cannot be given to the Corps commanded by Col. Morgan consisting of his* [[object Object]] *Regiment, and the light infantry of the* [[object Object]] *under Major Dearborn. But it would be* [[object Object]] *not to say that the whole body organized* [[object Object]] *the Honor & applause due to such exalted Merit. The Night after the action the heavy took part in the strong entrenched camp upon their loſs. Genl. Lincoln, whose decision was opposite to the heavy, going in the Afternoon to direct a cannonade to annoy their Camp, received a Musket Ball in his Leg which shattered the Bone. This has deprived me of the Assistance of one of the best officers as well as Men. His Loss at this Time* [[object Object]] *too much regretted. I am in Hopes his* [[object Object]] *be saved.*

The 9th at midnight the heavy quitted their entrenchments & retired to Saratoga. Early in the Morning of the 9th I [[object Object]] *the enclosed letter from Genl Burgoyne acquainting me that he left his whole Hospital to my protection, in which are 300 wounded officers & soldiers. Brigadier* [[object Object]] *Brigadr Genl Frazer who commanded the flying army of the heavy was killed the 7th* [[object Object]] *At one o'clock in the Morning of the 10th I* [[object Object]] *the enclosed letter from Genl Burgoyne with Lady Harriet Ackland. That morning as soon as the army could be properly put in Motion, I marched in Pursuit of the heavy and arrived here in* [[object Object]] *and found the heavy had taken* [[object Object]] *the opposite side of the (unclear) Hill in a entrenched camp which they occupied upon their advancing down the Country. The heavy have burnt all the houses before them as they (unclear). The extensive Buildings and Mills & belonging Major Genl Schuyler are also laid in ashes.*

This shameful Behavior [[object Object]] *by sending a Drum with the enclosed* [[object Object]] *to Genl Burgoyne. I am* [[object Object]] *your Excellency that* [[object Object]] *a deep Root in the Royal* [[object Object]] *particularly among the Germans who come to us in shoals. I am so (unclear) pressed on every side with Buiness that is impossible for me to be more* [[object Object]] *more particular now, but I hope in a few days to have Leisure to acquaint your Excellency with every Circumstance at present omitted.*

I am with great respect your Excellency's most obd hble Ser.
Horatio Gates

His Excellency John Hancock, Esq.
[[object Object]]

Copy of Letter from Horatio Gates Campt at Saratoga
Oct. 12, 1777

The Battle of Saratoga had a couple of social impacts that would affect several people over the course of the war.

As a consequence of their siding with the British, the Bemis and Freeman families lost their property at the war's end and moved to Canada, as did many Loyalists whose property was dispossessed. The act of taking property from Loyalists continued for the course of the war. At its end, families lost

Left: Interior of the Neilson house at Saratoga National Battlefield Park.

Right: Interior of the Neilson house at Saratoga National Battlefield Park, angled to show more details of the interior.

huge tracts of land and other property as a consequence of being on the wrong side of the war.

Another social impact of the war was the publication of private diaries, which provided an accurate portrayal of the events of the Revolution and the people who were involved in it. One diary published at the end of the war was that of the Baroness von Riedesel. It provided historians with a unique look into the past, from a woman of standing who sided with the British. Her diary not only told of the events at the Battle of Saratoga but also recounted the British retreat from Saratoga to Boston, where the Riedesels would live for a year before moving to the South, where the military action was light and the baroness and her children would be out of harm's way. The diary of the baroness, as well as that of Lady Harriet Acland, wife of John Dyke Acland, an officer in Burgoyne's army, give firsthand accounts of the Saratoga Campaign. The entries describe a war coming to an end, fear for loved ones caught up in battle and women and families coping with the hell of war. Soldiers' and officers' accounts of the war from both sides of the conflict are plentiful, but the diaries of two Loyalist women offer

Top: Artillery at Saratoga National Battlefield Park.

Bottom: A single cannon at Saratoga National Battlefield Park.

different perspectives—those of wives and mothers, not as combatants or those educated in warfare.

Another major impact of the Battle of Saratoga was the end of accepted rules of engagement. Colonel Daniel Morgan's group of Kentucky Riflemen were known for using guerrilla tactics—they hid in trees around the battlefield and shot at British commanding officers, leaving soldiers without leaders. Such actions had been frowned upon in previous battles and previous wars, but they proved very useful to the Americans and were continued during the remainder of the war.

The famous boot monument of Saratoga National Battlefield Park.

The Battle of Saratoga, and the Saratoga Campaign as a whole, was a turning point in the Revolution. The success of the American forces at these battles drove the British forces from fighting the Americans in New York for a time and showed the world that the Americans, although not educated in the ways of war to the extent the British military was, could hold their own and be successful. From the victory at the Battle of Saratoga came agreements between the French and the Americans and the Dutch and the Americans. Those European nations pledged to provide the fledgling army with men, ships and money to fight the remainder of the war, and this turned the tide in the Americans' favor.

With their failure to take New York and split the colonies in half as intended, the British left New York for a time and focused their energy on battles elsewhere.

THE VICTORY AT THE Battles of Saratoga was the turning point of the American War for Independence for the Patriots. The rebel underdogs beat a major global superpower, drawing international interest to their cause.

8

INTERNATIONAL INTEREST

When we think of the American Revolution and the international interest that was generated by the war, we typically think only of the French, who assisted the Continental army with arms, armaments, munitions, manpower and money. But other countries had a stake in the outcome of the war. We should think of the war in two terms: as a sort of civil war, and as one battlefront in a major world war, because that's exactly what the war was.

The American War for Independence can be viewed as a civil war in the sense that it tore familial and friend groups apart. People were more or less forced to choose sides, whether they agreed with the war or not, and the side they chose dictated how others associated with them. This could, and often did, affect businesses negatively as well, as people wanted to support only those who believed in the same cause they did. This sort of civil war division can be seen in popular culture, such as the 2000 film *The Patriot* starring Mel Gibson, and in the middle-grade 1974 book *My Brother Sam Is Dead* by James Lincoln Collier and Christopher Collier. Even history itself backs the idea that the American War for Independence was a civil war. In 1775, it was called a civil war until South Carolina chief justice William Henry Drayton called the war the "American Revolution" in 1776, a term that has stuck for nearly 250 years. The American War for Independence was also seen as a civil war because most Americans at the time still thought of

Left: The Marquis de Lafayette in the uniform of a major general of the Continental army, by Charles Willson Peale, between 1779 and 1780. *Wikimedia Commons.*

Right: Anne-César de La Luzerne. *Photo credit: The Miriam and Ira D. Wallach Division of Art, Prints and Photographs: Print Collection, The New York Public Library Digital Collections.*

themselves as English subjects, and one-third of those who fought in the war were Loyalists—those born in North America who were loyal to the mother country of Great Britain.

The Revolutionary War, though, was also one battlefront in a world war, even though, when the general public thinks about world wars, they think of the global conflicts in the 1910s and 1930s–40s. During the American Revolution, Spain, France and the Netherlands helped the Continental army and Continental Congress. France famously sent numerous envoys and ambassadors to what would become the United States, among them the Marquis de Lafayette and the Chevalier de La Luzerne, for diplomatic reasons as well as to provide the fledgling country with money, arms and other benefits. Spain also provided manpower and arms to the Continental army, and the Netherlands traded weapons and other goods to the Americans.

Even moving away from what those other nations provided to the rebellious American colonists, historians and nonhistorians alike must take into account *why* those other nations stepped into the war arena. France and Spain were both monarchies that detested the idea of democracy (and beginning in 1789, France would have its own revolution), and the Netherlands—at the time of the Revolution known as the Dutch Republic—was more interested in trade. Looking into these facts shows that nations weren't interested in the war because they held similar ideologies as the colonists. What the leaders of these countries were interested in was free trade, and they were willing to go to war against their competitor, Great Britain, to increase trade and economic dominance. For these three countries, the war was about profit. At the end of the war, with an American victory, the British experienced an economic downturn (adding to the British Empire's existing struggle following the global Seven Years' War), and the Americans were free to trade with nations rather than being limited to their former mercantile mother country. This opened up new trade opportunities in North America for the French, Spanish and Dutch.

There is no doubt that these three countries played a major role in the American victory, especially with the French helping the Americans at the Battle of Yorktown. But what happened after the war to make the American War for Independence a global conflict?

For the British, French, Spanish and Dutch, the fighting didn't end at Yorktown in 1781 but instead ended around 1783. After the American victory, France and Spain planned to invade Britain, both wishing to win back land that had been seized by the superpower. For the Spanish, this meant Gibraltar. The French sought to regain their former landholdings in India lost in the Seven Years' War. Britain, however, managed to avoid invasion and came out on top of France and Spain. The final battle in this conflict took place in Cuddalore in southeastern India near the Bay of Bengal.

In 1783, Britain negotiated separate treaties with the fledgling United States, France, Spain and the Dutch Republic. The treaties resulted in Britain maintaining its superior naval forces and the American colonies gaining their independence. France regained some of the prestige it had lost as a result of the Seven Years' War, and Spain was guaranteed landholdings and trade routes in the Americas.

Americans tend to have a very American-centric, practically narcissistic view of history, in which we are always the main character in the story. The Founding Fathers noted how paramount their allies were to the war effort, yet America as a whole has developed a sort of founding mythology of untrained farmers and merchants rising up against a major global superpower, struggling against the difficulties of war and needing some help only toward the end. According to Dr. David K. Allison, the chief curator emeritus of the Smithsonian National Museum of American history:

> *Our nation was formed from colonies of other nations, and the native peoples they encountered in North America. The revolution that gave us independence was in fact a world war, and battles fought elsewhere determined the outcome as much as what happened in North America. Without allies, the colonies would never have gained their freedom. Since then, development and prosperity have always been shaped by our relations with other countries, as they continue to be today. American history without the perspective of its international context leads us to false and dangerous perceptions of who we really are.*

To many, the American War for Independence is a story of how a group of ragtag, barely trained volunteers rose up against the oppressive government that had them bound in mercantilist servitude. The actions of the British and their Loyalist forces as well as their Native American allies take a back seat to the heroism of the men who fought and died for the notion of a nation free from monarchical rule. And even the actions of the Americans' allies take a back seat to the heroism of those who were born on this continent. As Americans, we must realize that there are more players involved in the American War for Independence than just those who won and who lost, as both sides had allies that played major roles in the war. And we must recognize the war for what it was—both a civil war and a world war. We must also realize that if we ignore the actions of one side, we ignore half of the war, and thus we ignore half of the story of how we won our independence. Everyone's story is important, even if we sometimes struggle to see that as a fact. No one is insignificant.

AFTERWORD

The year 2020, which brought monumental and devastating change to so many, was a year that I won't forget, for so many reasons. It was a year in which I was coming to terms with the end of my marriage to my high school sweetheart in 2019, struggled with the anxieties that come with a new relationship after not dating for years, endured hardships at work that led to the impromptu decision to quit and work a temporary job while applying for positions that would lead to a career, moving and having to navigate daily life during a widespread global pandemic (masks and hand sanitizers being used constantly and various grocery shortages...oh my!). Most important, the year was also when I came into my own as a historian, with the publication of my first book with The History Press and my blog reaching over 121,000 views before the year's end.

In 2021, life changed significantly for me again, as I was approved to write a second book (this book) for The History Press. I also started a history podcast, was a guest on other history podcasts, was present for in-person events and book signings and, at the tail end of the year, found myself teaching at the middle-school level at a private school in Upstate New York.

As a result of the pandemic, my interest in local history increased. I'd have long stretches of time where I wasn't needed for work, so I spent my time researching anything that I found of interest. I was also able to connect with other history professionals and learn more about the American Revolution, the Civil War and other historical topics. The National Park Service posted information about battles on social media, local historical societies were posting on social media and historians turned to YouTube to share their knowledge with others. It was a great period of learning for me.

In the early days and weeks of the quarantine that affected the majority of Americans (I say this because different groups of people were affected differently), I saw memes on my social media feeds about living through historical events. One meme I saw multiple times said something along the lines of, "I'm living through a major historical period of time and what am I doing with my life? Laundry, mostly." Countless times, I saw people ask, "What were normal people doing during times of historical changes?" They were simply living their regular, everyday lives. To quote John W. Gardner, "History never looks like history when you're living through it." That can be said for the people of the past as well, not just for us.

I'm a social historian who utilizes the bottom-up approach made famous by Howard Zinn, E.P. Thompson, Staughton Lynd and others. A lot of what I do is research about what the average person was doing in a given period, and how I and other social historians do this is through primary documents.

What is the bottom-up approach to history? It is an approach that examines the lives of ordinary people and often marginalized groups as its subjects and concentrates on their experiences and perspectives. This approach challenges the mainstream versions of the past, proving that history isn't made only by these great men and women but by average people as well. It also recognizes that the lives of these average people should be regarded not merely as sources of facts but also as interpreters of what happened.

The thing I love most about history, as a social historian, is that anyone can be a historian, that we are all makers of history as well as being made by history—both our personal histories and what happens in the larger world around us.

I'm a firm believer that all history is local. It's this belief that led me to write about the American Revolution as it happened in New York for my graduate thesis, which led to my first book, which led to this book…and which will hopefully lead to more books. For many people, history is something that happens in faraway places, not places tucked into the mountains of their home state and certainly not (sometimes literally) in their own backyards. But local history is incredibly important.

When we learn about history in school, we often learn about the major events and individuals, dramatic events that affected our country or the world on a grand scale. But these events had local impacts as well, and keeping history in a local context can help us understand the lives of everyday individuals, the people who are like us. Localizing history helps shape who we are, even if we may not realize its impact. Local history shapes local culture, and this affects who we are.

I'm also a firm believer that all of us can contribute to our local history. We can keep journals and write about our own lives for future generations to use as primary sources to learn about the past. Or we can research through primary, secondary and tertiary sources and share our findings in a variety of ways to ensure that the stories of the past, especially the little-known and previously unknown stories, get passed down to the next generations.

For many people at the time of the American Revolutionary War, the news of anti-British protests, the news of the fighting, the sight of soldiers in their towns and cities, the steep prices for goods and the lack of some items as rations affected the populace were all a necessary part of life. But how the war affected the people, soldiers and civilians alike is a part of our history now. For them, it was just the status quo.

During the early days of the pandemic in 2020, and multiple times on social media since then, I've seen calls for action from individual historians, state and national archives and museums, urging people to write down their experiences for future generations. This simple act would increase the historiography of both local history and social history. Those in our nation's past have done that—writing their experiences, maintaining military records and land grants and other important documents. All of those stories are important.

The idea of social history, of taking a bottom-up approach to history, shows the importance of the individuals involved in the life-altering actions that happened in their time that continue to affect us today—and maintains my belief stated near the end of the last chapter of this book: Everyone's story is important.

The individuals in this book may be little known or unknown to some. The actions described may be little known or unknown to some. But that doesn't diminish the importance of those Loyalist individuals and actions. Without these actions, the American forces during the American Revolution and the allies who joined them wouldn't have risen to the occasion of securing freedom and founding our country.

Appendix

TIMELINES BY CHAPTER

Chapter 1

November 1, 1765: Stamp Act enacted after passage in Parliament in March; protests begin; Stamp Act Riot occurs in New York City.
May 10, 1773: Tea Act passes in Parliament.
April 18, 1774: New York Tea Party.
November 7, 1775: Lord Dunmore issues his proclamation.
June 30, 1779: Sir Henry Clinton issues his Philipsburg Proclamation.

Chapter 4

June 22, 1774: Quebec Act of 1774 passes in Parliament.
August 25, 1775: Quebec Campaign begins.
September 17, 1775: Attack of Fort St. John.
December 31, 1775: Siege of Quebec.

Chapter 5

May 10, 1775: American forces take over Fort Ticonderoga.
December 31, 1775: Siege of Quebec.
October 11, 1776: Battle of Valcour Island.
July 5, 1777: Americans evacuate Fort Ticonderoga.

Chapter 6

Mid-1760s: Brothers Edward and Ebenezer Jessup move from Dutchess County, New York, to Albany, New York, to participate in land speculation.
1760s–75: The Jessups become associated with Sir William Johnson and the Mohawk Nation and purchase large tracts of land that become the towns of Lake Luzerne, Corinth, Hadley, Warrensburg, Thurman, Chestertown and Johnsburg.
1763: Edward and Ebenezer begin lumbering operations in what would become the towns of Lake Luzerne and Corinth.
Winter 1775: Colonists begin destroying property belonging to the Jessups, burning the mills, destroying a ferry and ransacking the Jessup homestead.
Summer 1776: Edward and Ebenezer lead a party of eighty Loyalist troops to Crown Point to aid the British forces stationed there.
May 6, 1777: Thirty-one Loyalists are captured on or near the Jessup Patent. Edward Jessup flees, following the Hudson River, to meet his brother and General John Burgoyne encamped at Willsborough Falls.
Summer–October 1777: The Jessup brothers participate in Burgoyne's Saratoga Campaign and are present for the British surrender.
September 24, 1777: Battle of Diamond Island.

Chapter 7

July 5, 1777: Americans evacuate Fort Ticonderoga.
July 7, 1777: Battle of Hubbardton.
July 8, 1777: Battle of Fort Anne.
July 27, 1777: Murder of Jane McCrea, a young Loyalist woman.
July 29, 1777: British forces take Fort Edward and Fort George.
August 6, 1777: Battle of Oriskany.
August 15, 1777: Battle of Bennington.
September 19, 1777: Battle of Freeman's Farm.
September 20–October 7, 1777: Battle of Bemis Heights.
October 8, 1777: British surrender after Battle of Saratoga.

BIBLIOGRAPHY

Documents and Exhibits

Arnold, Isaac N. "Benedict Arnold at Saratoga: Reply to John Austin Stevens, and new evidence of Mr. Bancroft's error." New York State Library, 1880.

Bielinski, Stefan. *Benjamin Lattimore.* New York State Museum. https://exhibitions.nysm.nysed.gov.

Boonshoft, Mark. "Dispossessing Loyalists and Redistributing Property in Revolutionary New York." New York Public Library, September 19, 2016. www.nypl.org/blog.

Gates, Horatio, "Letter to John Hancock, about Battle of Freeman's Farm and casualties." Digital Public Library of America. https://dp.la.

"Henry Knox to George Washington, December 17, 1775." The Gilder Lehrman Institute of American History. https://www.gilderlehrman.org.

Makos, Isaac. "The Siege of Fort Ticonderoga: 1777." American Battlefield Trust. https://www.battlefields.org.

Philipsburg Proclamation. Archived from the original. Black Loyalist Heritage Centre. www.blackloyalist.com.

Schuyler, Philip. "To George Washington from Major Philip Schuyler, 7 July, 1777." National Archives. Founders Documents. https://founders.archives.gov.

Seelinger, Matthew. "Buying Time: The Battle of Valcour Island." National Museum of the United States Army. https://armyhistory.org.

The Stamp Act. Published 1765 in London. The Gilder Lehrman Institute of American History. GLC03562.11. https://www.gilderlehrman.org.

Books

Allison, David K., and Larrie D. Ferreiro. *The American Revolution: A World War*. Washington, DC: Smithsonian Books, 2018.

Bennett, David. *A Few Lawless Vagabonds: Ethan Allen, the Republic of Vermont, and the American Revolution*. Philadelphia: Casemate Publishers, 2014.

Boehlert, Paul A. *The Battle of Oriskany and General Nicholas Herkimer: Revolution in the Mohawk Valley*. Charleston, SC: The History Press, 2013.

Breen, T.H. *American Insurgents, American Patriots: The Revolution of the People*. New York: Hill and Wang, 2010.

Campbell, William W. *The Annals of Tryon County, or The Border Warfare of New York during the Revolution*. New York: J&J Harper, 1831.

Charles-Edwards, T., and B. Richardson. *They Saw It Happen: An Anthology of Eyewitness Accounts of Events in British History 1689–1897*. Oxford, UK: Blackwell, 1958.

Countryman, Edward. *A People in Revolution: The American Revolution and Political Society in New York, 1760–1790*. New York: Johns Hopkins University Press, 1981.

Ellis, David M., James A. Frost and William B. Fink. *New York: The Empire State*. Englewood Cliffs, NJ: Prentice-Hall, 1980.

Jones, Thomas. *History of New York during the Revolutionary War and of the Leading Events in the Other Colonies at That Period*. New York: New-York Historical Society, 1879.

Kelsay, Isabel Thompson. *Joseph Brant: A Man of Two Worlds, 1743–1807*. Syracuse, NY: Syracuse University Press, 1984.

Ketchum, Richard M. *Saratoga: Turning Point of America's Revolutionary War*. New York: Henry Holt, 1997.

Logusz, Michael O. *With Musket and Tomahawk: The Mohawk Valley Campaign in the Wilderness War of 1777*. Havertown, PA: Casemate Publishers, 2012.

———. *With Musket and Tomahawk: The Saratoga Campaign in the Wilderness War of 1777*. Havertown, PA: Casemate Publishers, 2010.

Lowenthal, Larry, ed. *Days of Siege: A Journal of the Siege of Fort Stanwix*. N.p.: Eastern Acorn Press, 1983.

Luzader, John F. *Saratoga: A Military History of the Decisive Campaign of the American Revolution*. New York: Savas Beatie, 2008.

National Reporter System. *The New York State Supplement with Key Number Annotations, Volume 134. New York State Reporter, Volume 168. Containing the Decisions of the Supreme and Lower Courts of Record of New York State with Table of Statutes Construed.* April 15–May 27, 1912. St. Paul, NY: West Publishing Company, 1912.

Pancake, John S. *1777: The Year of the Hangman*. Tuscaloosa: University of Alabama Press, 1977.

Sails and Steam in the Mountains: A Maritime and Military History of Lake George and Lake Champlain. Fleischmanns, NY: Purple Mountain Press, 1992.

Smith, William. *The Candid Retrospect: Or the American War Examined, by Whig Principles*. Charlestown, SC: John Wells, 1780.

Snow, Dean. *1777: Tipping Point at Saratoga*. New York: Oxford University Press, 2016.

Washington, Ida H., and Paul A. Washington. *Carleton's Raid*. Weybridge, VT: Cherry Tree Books, 1977.

Watt, Gavin K. *The Burning of the Valleys: Daring Raids from Canada against the New York Frontier in the Fall of 1780*. Toronto: Dundurn, 1997.

Wilson, David. *The Life of Jane McCrea: With an Account of Burgoyne's Expedition in 1777*. New York: Baker, Goodwin & Company, 1853.

Wood, Gordon S. *The Radicalism of the American Revolution*. New York: Random House, 1991.

Articles

American Revolution. "Frederica de Riedesel." www.americanrevolution.org.

———. "Harriet Ackland." www.americanrevolution.org.

American Revolutionary War. "The Battle of Cherry Valley (Massacre)." https://revolutionarywar.us.

Ayres, Edward. "African Americans and the American Revolution." The American Revolution Museum at Yorktown. https://www.historyisfun.org.

Bellico, Russell. "Revisiting the 1777 Battle of Diamond Island." *Lake George (NY) Mirror*, July 12, 2019.

Bluhm, Raymond K. "Siege of Fort Ticonderoga." Encyclopedia Britannica. https://www.britannica.com.

Central Intelligence Agency. "Intelligence throughout History: The Capture of Fort Ticonderoga, 1775." April 30, 2013.

Cornish, Paul. "Quebec Act of 1774." The First Amendment Encyclopedia. Middle Tennessee State University. https://www.mtsu.edu/first-amendment.

Edgerton, Samuel Y., Jr. "The Murder of Jane McCrea: The Tragedy of an American Tableau d'Histoire." *Art Bulletin* 47, no. 4 (December 1965): 481–92.

EyeWitness to History. "Battle at Lexington Green, 1775: The British Perspective." 2010. www.eyewitnesstohistory.com.

Fort Haldimand. "Fort Haldimand: History." http://www.forthaldimand.com.

Fort Stanwix National Monument. "The Clinton-Sullivan Campaign of 1779." National Park Service. https://www.nps.gov.

Friends of Bennington Battle Monument. "The Battle of Bennington: Turning Point of the American Revolution". www.benningtonbattleonument.com.

George, Alice. "The American Battlefield Was Just One Battlefront in a Huge World War." *Smithsonian Magazine*, June 28, 2018.

Glidden, G. William. "The Jessups, Adirondack Land Barons." Warren County Historical Society. February 1, 2015. http://www.warrencountyhistoricalsociety.org.

Hickman, Kennedy. "American Revolution: Siege of Fort Ticonderoga (1777)." ThoughtCo.com, March 17, 2017. https://www.thoughtco.com.

Historian at Saratoga. "Baroness Described the 1st Battle of Saratoga." September 22, 2016. https://historianatsaratoga.wordpress.coma.

History.com. "Poor Leadership Leads to Cherry Valley Massacre." November 11, 2009. https://www.history.com.

Mohawk Valley Region. "American Revolution in the Mohawk Valley Region." Path through History. https://www.mohawkvalleyhistory.com.

Saratoga County Chamber of Commerce. "The Battle of Saratoga". www.saratoga.org.

Sawyer, William. "The 1777 Siege of Fort Schuyler." National Park Service. https://www.nps.gov.

Venture, Bruce. "The Forgotten Battle of Diamond Island on Lake George." Adirondack Almanack, June 17, 2015. https://www.adirondackalmanack.com.

Warren, John. "Why Fort Anne's Battle Hill Is Significant." *New York State History Blog*, April 25, 2012. http://newyorkhistoryblog.org.

Wuertenberg, Nathan. "Quebec Campaign." George Washington's Mount Vernon. https://www.mountvernon.org.

ABOUT THE AUTHOR

MARIE DANIELLE ANNETTE WILLIAMS is an educator and independent historian living in Upstate New York. She received her bachelor of arts degree in social studies adolescent education from The College of Saint Rose in Albany, New York, in 2014 and received her master of arts degree in American history from Southern New Hampshire University in Manchester, New Hampshire, in 2018. When Marie isn't teaching or writing, she's researching for her blog, *The Half-Pint Historian Blog*, and podcast, *The Half-Pint Historian Podcast*; drinking more tea and coffee than she should; spending time with her partner and their cat; and overall living her best life.

Visit us at
www.historypress.com